GOD'S YOUNG CHURCH

BOOKS BY WILLIAM BARCLAY
Published by The Westminster Press

God's Young Church
The King and the Kingdom
The First Three Gospels
Fishers of Men
Turning to God: A Study of Conversion
    in the Book of Acts and Today
Many Witnesses, One Lord
The All-Sufficient Christ:
    Studies in Paul's Letter to the Colossians
The Promise of the Spirit
Train Up a Child:
    Educational Ideals in the Ancient World
Daily Study Bible

GOD'S YOUNG CHURCH

by
WILLIAM BARCLAY

THE WESTMINSTER PRESS
Philadelphia

Published by The Westminster Press ®
Philadelphia, Pennsylvania

PRINTED IN THE UNITED STATES OF AMERICA

CONTENTS

Foreword

This book consists of parts of two Bible class handbooks: *God's Men, God's Church and God's Law;* and *God's Law, God's Servants and God's Men.* These handbooks were never available for general sale and use, and at the end of their own year they simply ceased to be. I am most grateful to The Saint Andrew Press and The Westminster Press for the decision to revive them, and to make them available for a wider public. And I am exceedingly grateful to my close friend, the Rev. James Martin, B.D., of High Carntyne Church, Glasgow, for making the necessary selections and for preparing the books for the press.

It is my hope and my prayer that this book will prove of some use to those whose task it is to teach the Bible material and to those whose joy it is to study the Bible.

WILLIAM BARCLAY

Glasgow University,
February 1970

ACKNOWLEDGEMENTS

The author and publisher acknowledge with appreciation permission to quote from the following copyright sources:

The Society of Authors, for the Bernard Shaw Estate, for the extracts from Scenes IV and V of *Saint Joan* by Bernard Shaw. Mrs. Bambridge and the Macmillan Companies for the first and last verses of "The Thousandth Man" by Rudyard Kipling, taken from *Rewards and Fairies*.

PART 1: GOD'S CHURCH

Chapter 1

THE CHURCH'S COMMISSION

Acts 1:8 tells us the orders of Jesus to His men before He ascended to His Father. He said, "You shall be my witnesses in Jerusalem and in all Judea and Samaria and to the end of the earth." That is just another way of putting that great commandment with which Matthew's Gospel closes and which is the marching order of the Church—"Go therefore and make disciples of all nations" (Matthew 28:19).

So it was Jesus' commandment that His followers should be *witnesses* to Him. First, then, we have to ask, "What is a witness?" A witness is a person who says, "This is true and I know it." The great characteristic of a witness is that he must speak at first hand. If we are ever witnesses in a court of law we will be allowed to repeat only what we ourselves have personally seen and heard and what we know from experience is true. If, then, we are to be witnesses for Jesus the first essential is that we should know Jesus at first hand. If we are going to spread the gospel of Jesus abroad we must ourselves really and truly know what that gospel is.

The Necessity of Thought

If we are to have this first-hand knowledge two things are necessary. First, we must think things out for ourselves. We must always be asking the question, "What does this mean and what does it mean for me and what must I do about it?" Kipling has a poem in which he writes:

> I keep six honest serving-men,
>   (They taught me all I knew),
> Their names are What and Why and When
>   And How and Where and Who.

And then he goes on to say,

> I send them over land and sea,
> I send them east and west.

These words are good serving men. If you ask someone the question "Why should I believe this?" and the person answers you, "Because I said it," that is always a bad reason. We should not believe things merely because anyone told us them, but because we have thought them out for ourselves.

Once, not long before He took the road to Jerusalem and the Cross, Jesus asked His friends a most important question. At the time He wanted to be quite sure that there were some few people who knew who He really was, because He knew that very soon His enemies were going to kill Him, and He did not want to see everything go for nothing. So He asked them, "Who do men say that the Son of man is?" And they passed on to Him the various opinions and verdicts which were current. But then He finished by asking them the question, "Who do you say that I am?" (Matthew 16:13-15). It was never enough to tell what others thought. They had to think it out for themselves, and we must do the same if we are to be witnesses who can say, "I know that this is true".

The Necessity of Experience

But even more than the necessity of thinking things out there is the necessity of actually knowing and meeting Jesus for ourselves. The greatest of all mistakes is to think of Jesus as a figure in a book, as someone who lived and died and who is gone and whose story we tell. Jesus is alive for evermore and we can meet Him as we can meet any friend. And it is only when we really know Jesus in that sense that we can be absolutely and completely sure of Him. If that be so why do we not meet Him oftener than we do? Very likely the reason is that we do not give ourselves a chance to meet Him, nor Him a chance to meet us.

In George Bernard Shaw's play, *Saint Joan*, there is a conversation between the Dauphin of France and Joan. Joan heard voices which came to her direct from God and told her what to do. She was always hearing these voices. The Dauphin was annoyed about it all. "Oh, your voices, your voices," he said, "Why don't the voices come to me? I am King, not you." And Joan answered him, "They do come to you, but you do not hear them. You have not sat in the field in the evening listening for them. When the angelus rings you cross yourself and have done with it; but if you prayed from your heart, and listened to the thrilling of the bells in the air after they stop ringing, you would hear the voices as well as I do." The Dauphin did not hear the voices because he did not give himself a chance to hear them.

In Amos there is a wonderful text which is still more wonderful when we know what it really means. Amos asks the question of men and God. "Do two walk together, unless they have made an appointment?" (Amos 3:3). People do not meet unless they have made an arrangement to meet. There should be some part of each day which we set aside to think about Jesus and to speak to Him and wait for His presence. It need not be long; it can be any time in the day and anywhere. When we do that we will really meet Him and then we will be real witnesses because we will be able to say beyond all shadow of doubt, "I know".

Witnessing at Home

Now let us look where Jesus' men were to be witnesses. The command was that they were to be witnesses in Jerusalem, and in all Judea, and in Samaria, and to the end of the earth (Acts 1:8). It is as if they were to take Jerusalem as a centre and then draw a series of ever widening concentric circles until the widest circle of all took in the whole wide world. They were to start in *Jerusalem*. That is to say, they were to start at *home*. They say that charity begins at home; our Christian witness very definitely begins at home. Once in the country of the Gadarenes, Jesus cured a man who was violently mad. When the man was cured naturally his heart overflowed with gratitude to Jesus and he asked Jesus to let him come with Him and follow Him all the time. Jesus answered, "Go home to your friends, and tell them how much the Lord has done for you" (Mark 5:19).

There is no better place to practise being a Christian than at home. Very many of us misuse our homes altogether. We think of our homes as places where we can be, as we say, ourselves. Too often that means that we think that we have a right to be as cross and bad-tempered and irritable and selfish as we like in our homes and that we can treat our nearest and dearest with a discourtesy and a lack of consideration that we would never dream of showing to strangers or to people we do not know very well. We can and must and ought to begin to demonstrate Christianity in our own homes. In them we will find all the chances we need to be as unselfish, as kind, as forgiving, as thoughtful and as considerate as a Christian ought to be.

Witnessing in our own Country

Next Jesus' men were to go on to *Judea*, that is to say they were to be witnesses in *their own country*. W. S. Gilbert has two biting lines about,

> The idiot who praises, with enthusiastic tone,
> All centuries but this, and every country but his own.

There are some people who are always praising all the times of the world's history except the one in which they live and who are always pointing out how much better every country is than the one in which they live. It is a first duty to try to make our own country a Christian country. How can we do that? We can do it by taking our Christianity with us into every sphere of life. One of the gravest mistakes we can make is to divide life into two compartments and to label one sacred and the other secular and to think that we serve God in Church and that we can forget God and leave Him behind us when we go into the world. Just because every moment of life is lived in God's presence, every moment of life should be an act of worship. There is a Latin proverb which says, *Laborare est orare*, to work is to pray. A man was once about to buy a house from a builder who was a really

Christian man; he bought the house without even seeing it. Someone said to him, "Was that not a risky thing to do?" He answered, "Not at all, that man builds his Christianity into his houses." When we go out to work we will go a long way towards making this a Christian country if we insist on taking our Christian principles with us into every part of life and in working in the utter certainty that every second of life is seen by God.

Witnessing to our Enemies

Next Jesus' men were to go on to *Samaria*. Now that was really surprising. The Jews were bitter enemies of the Samaritans and the Samaritans hated the Jews. "Jews have no dealings with Samaritans" (John 4:9). But this good news was to be brought even to people who were regarded as enemies. The truth, of course, is that the real Christian should not regard any man as his enemy. One of the great "ifs" of history is the question of what might have happened if the western peoples had sent abroad missionaries of the gospel instead of armies of war. In his book, *Then and Now*, Dr. John Foster tells of what someone has called "the greatest might-have-been in the history of the Church". In the year 1271 Kublai Khan was the ruler of the greatest empire that has ever been known. It stretched from the Ural Mountains to the Himalayas and from the China Sea to the River Danube. In that year he sent a letter to Pope Gregory the Tenth in which he said, "You shall go to your High Priest and shall pray him on our behalf to send me a hundred men skilled in your religion . . . and so I shall be baptised and when I shall be baptised all my barons and great men will be baptised, and then their subjects will receive baptism, and so there will be more Christians here than there are in your parts." This letter was sent through Nicolo and Maffeo Polo who were to be his ambassadors to the Pope and the result of it was that Pope Gregory did precisely nothing. Not for another eighteen years were missionaries despatched and they were far too few and by that time the whole situation had changed. If that chance had been seized there might have been no war in the

Far East, no war in Korea, no such thing as Communism; but at that time the Church failed. There is only one real way to destroy our enemies and that is to make them our friends; and we can only do that when we persuade them also to accept that gospel which alone can unite men into one.

Witnessing throughout all the World

Finally the witness of Jesus' men was to go out to *the end of the earth*. Jesus said "I, when I am lifted up from the earth, will draw all men to myself" (John 12:32). Paul dreamed of the day when at the name of Jesus every knee should bow and every tongue confess Him Lord (Philippians 2:10, 11). It is God's aim that everyone should know Him and love Him and so there is laid on us His people the duty of sending out our missionaries to the end of the earth to tell men the story of Jesus. Someone has put it this way.

> He has no hands but our hands
>   To do His work today;
> He has no feet but our feet
>   To lead men in His way;
> He has no voice but our voice
>   To tell men how He died;
> He has no help but our help
>   To lead men to His side.

The Christian Church can never be content until the last man in the world knows the story of Jesus; and so we by our prayers and by our giving must do all we can to help on that work.

The Christian Witness

It is our duty to be witnesses for Christ. To be that we must think things out and, above all, we must meet with Jesus until we can say, "I know that this is true". That witness must start at home; it must go out throughout our own land; it must be given even to those who are regarded as our enemies; and in the end it must go out to the end of the earth.

QUESTIONS FOR DISCUSSION

1. What things do we most need to talk over and to think over together?

2. How can a man bring his Christian witness into his day's work?

3. What would you say to a man who said that he did not believe in Missions?

Chapter 2

THE CHARACTERISTICS OF THE CHURCH

Acts 2:41-47 is one of the most interesting and important passages in the whole New Testament, because in these few verses there are summed up the characteristics which marked the early Church. We do well to look at them and to study them, not only that we may know and understand what the early Church was like, but also that we may reproduce them in our own lives and in our own Churches. Let us then look at these characteristics one by one.

A Learning Church

First and foremost, that early Church was *a learning Church*. Verse 42 tells us how they kept listening to the teaching of the apostles. We must always remember how people came into the Church in those early days. There were no Church buildings and no highly organised Church as we know it. A great deal of their preaching was done in the open air, at the street corner and in the city squares. If someone had a larger house than usual he would lend a room in that house for a meeting of the Christians on the Lord's Day. So what happened was this. A heathen would be going down the street of some town or city. He would see a little group of people listening to a man talking earnestly to them. He would go up to the group; if he was quite uninterested he would listen for a moment or two and pass on; if he was quite interested he might linger for a little; but if he was very interested and keenly attracted he would go up to the leader of the group and he would say, "Where can I find out more about this Jesus about whom you are speaking?" Then he would be directed to one of these house Churches where he would be more fully instructed in the faith. It is very important to note that his motive in coming to the Church was "Where can I find out more about Christ and Christianity?"

A real Church is always a learning Church and a real Christian is always a learning Christian. The great tragedy of so many people is that they stop learning so soon. When a census was being taken in Britain, the census papers had on them many questions which had to be answered. The famous journalist, Mr. Collie Knox, told how he refused to fill in an answer to one of the questions and when the official came to collect his paper he had quite an argument with him. The question was "At what age did you finish your education?" And Mr. Knox insisted that he could not answer that question because he had not finished it yet. Mr. Knox was right; a real man never stops learning. When Corot, the famous painter, was nearly seventy and when everyone would have said that he was an expert with nothing left to learn, he once said, "If God spares me for another ten years I think I may learn how to paint." The trouble with so many people's religion is that it is at a standstill. Paul spoke about the unsearchable riches of Christ. If a man learned for a thousand years there would still be wonder in Jesus that he had not exhausted. We should count it a wasted day when we have not learned something new; and to the end of life we should still be learning.

A Praying Church

But verse 42 tells us that not only did they persevere in listening to the apostles teach; they also persevered in *prayer*. These early Christians had a difficult time. They incurred the hatred and the dislike of the pagans; and often they had to suffer injuries and insults and sometimes persecutions. And they knew quite well that they could not face all this without the help which God could give them. When we pray we are putting ourselves in touch with the power of God. People used to say to Abraham Lincoln that he wasted time in prayer. His answer was "I would be the biggest fool in the world if I thought that I could sustain the difficulties of this

high office which has come to me for one day without the help
of someone who is greater and stronger than I." He knew
that he simply could not keep going without God's help.
They used to call St. Francis of Assisi the man who loved
mountains, because over and over again when he was faced
with some big task he would go away to some mountain top
to pray. That is what Jesus did. Often when we read the
gospels we read of Jesus going away to some mountain or
some other lonely place to speak to God, His Father. Lady
Astor told how she met a soldier who had been at Dunkirk
and how she asked him how they passed their time on the
beaches when they were waiting for the ships to take them off.
"Lady," he said, "I guess we prayed." If we want to live
life well we need more than our own strength to do so and we
get the extra strength through contact with God by the way
of prayer.

A Reverent Church

Verse 43 tells us two things about that early Church. First
of all it was *a reverent Church*. This verse says "Fear came
upon every soul." Often in the New Testament *fear* is not
the terror of being afraid; it is rather the awe which is reverence.
We should always be reverent when we come to Church because
in the Church in a very special sense we are in the presence
of God. Of course, it is true that, no matter where we are,
we are in the presence of God because this is God's world and
God is everywhere, but it is specially true in the Church. Now
just think of it. If we were summoned to Buckingham Palace
to the presence of the Queen, we would stand very straight
and behave very well and we would remember all the time that
this was the Queen's house and we were in the Queen's presence.
In Church we are in the presence of the King of Kings. To be
restless, fidgety, inattentive, to talk and to chatter and to
misbehave is not only an insult to the person who is speaking
or preaching, it is an insult to God. We must see to it that
in God's House our behaviour is always fit for the presence
of God.

A Church where things happened

But verse 43 also tells us that many wonders and signs were done by the apostles. The early Church was *a Church where things happened*. It was a Church where sick people were cured and where bad people were made good. In a real Church things still happen. There was once a man who had been a drunkard and who had ruined his own life and the life of his family through his weakness. He became a Christian, conquered his bad habits and became a good citizen and a good husband and father. Some of his work-mates used to tease him. "Surely you don't believe, do you, in the Bible and all that? For instance, surely you don't believe in miracles? You don't believe, do you, that Jesus turned water into wine?" He answered, "I'm no scholar and I don't know whether Jesus turned water into wine or not; but in my own house I've seen Him turn beer into furniture."

Jesus is still able to change people. One of the reasons why things do not happen is that we do not expect them to happen. A great saint gave good advice in a famous sentence, "Expect great things from God, attempt great things for God." And if we tried hard enough and if we trusted God enough, great things could and would happen even yet.

A Sharing Church

Verses 44 and 45 tell us a very lovely thing about that early Church. They tell us that it was *a sharing Church*. Those who were rich shared all they had with those who were poor. People in those days felt that they just could not possess too much whilst others possessed too little. In the early Church they had a very lovely custom. Every Sunday they had what they called the Love Feast. To that feast everyone brought something, just as he was able. They pooled everything that was brought and then they sat down to share it out together. At this feast all kinds of people were sitting together. Many of the early Christians were very poor; some of them were slaves. A slave's rations in Greece were a quart of meal a day with a few figs and olives and a little wine and vinegar. Very often this common meal on the Lord's Day was the only decent meal the slave got all week, and he only got it because in that early Church everyone shared with everyone else everything he had. If the spirit of Christ is really in us we will not be able to be happy if we see someone else in need and do not help him.

A Worshipping Church

Verse 46 tells us a number of characteristics of this early Church. It begins by telling us that these early Christians daily attended the Temple together. That is to say that early Church was *a worshipping Church*. We may put it this way— they never forgot to go to Church. There are many reasons for going to Church but let us think of only two. To go to Church is one of the best ways of showing our loyalty to Jesus. If every Saturday afternoon people see us going down the street to a certain football park, they know at once what team we support; and if every Sunday people see us go down the street and into the Church, they know at once what side we are on. If we want to demonstrate our loyalty to Jesus, there are few better ways of doing it than by faithfully entering His house on the Lord's Day. The second reason for going to Church is this. People often say that we do not need to go to Church, that we can worship God anywhere, that we can find God on the open road or the hilltop or beside the sea. Of course, that is true in one sense, but it is not the whole truth. Think of it this way. Suppose we go to a big concert; now suppose we were the only person in the hall or the theatre or suppose there were only one or two there besides ourselves— would we enjoy it just as well as if the hall were crowded? We would not, because half the thrill is to be one of a great audience and to hear the laughter of many people and share in their applause. Suppose we were to go to a big football match, a cup-tie, and we were the only person there or one of very few, would it be just as thrilling? Of course not. Part of the thrill comes from being one of a great crowd, all excited, all cheering and all supporting their team. Well, worship is something like that. One of the great things about coming to Church is that in Church we feel one of a great company. We share the singing and we share the prayers and we all listen together. We get far more out of that experience of being together than of being alone. A real Christian will be a worshipping Christian and will be faithful in his attendance at God's House.

The Characteristics of the Church

We must retain the remainder of the characteristics of the Church for the next chapter; but let us see just how far we have reached now. The early Church was *a learning Church*; we must count it a wasted day when we do not learn something we did not know before. The early Church was *a praying Church*; it knew that strength for daily life and living can be gained only by continual contact with God. The early Church was *a reverent* Church; in God's house we must behave as those who are in the presence of the King. The early Church was *a Church where things happened*; if we expect great things from God we will receive great things from Him. The early Church was *a sharing Church*; we can never be happy when we have too much and when others have too little. The early Church was *a worshipping Church*; we are missing something infinitely precious when we do not join with God's people in God's House.

QUESTIONS FOR DISCUSSION

1. What methods can we use always to keep on learning?

2. How can we teach ourselves to be reverent when we come to Church?

3. Do you think that attending a Church organisation is a substitute for attending Church?

Chapter 3

THE CHARACTERISTICS OF THE CHURCH (*contd.*)

A Brotherly Church

We have already seen some of the fine characteristics of the early Church but there are others and even greater to come. Acts 2:46 says that the Christians day by day broke bread in their homes. That gives us a picture of a Church which was *a real fellowship*. The Christians were friends with each other; they ate with each other and talked with each other and were happy together. They had what someone has called the "spirit of togetherness". When Nelson was sending home a despatch concerning one of his greatest victories he explained his victory by saying, "I had the happiness to command a band of brothers." The early Christians were a band of brothers. Christians should always be friends of one another. External differences of rank and wealth and place and position should not enter into the question at all. If a man's Christianity does not make him friendly it will not make him anything.

John Wesley was very definite about this. At one time in his life he thought of separating himself altogether from his fellow-men and of building himself a little cabin away on the moors and of spending all his life doing nothing but praying and meditating and thinking of God. But an older and a wiser person said to him, "God knows nothing of solitary religion." He tells how he talked with a good and serious person who said to him, "You must either find companions or make them; there is no such thing as going to heaven alone."

It has often been all too sadly true that Churches have been places where people argued and debated and disputed and sometimes even quarrelled with one another. When that happens a Church has ceased to be a Church in any real sense of the term. A true Church is a real fellowship where people are friends and where the members are one united band of brothers.

A Happy Church

This same verse (verse 46) goes on to say that they ate their meat with gladness. That is to say the early Church was *a happy Church*. Those early Christians were glad and they wanted everyone to know it. Far too often Christianity has been associated with gloom. Someone once described a preacher as preaching the gospel like a wireless announcer announcing a deep depression off Iceland. John Bunyan, in the days when he was still in the middle of doubts and fears and problems, describes how he once went down the street and heard some old women who were true Christians speak and he says of them, "Methinks they spoke as if joy did make them speak." Often Jesus spoke with a smile. Often He said something which must have made people laugh. There is His vivid humorous picture of the man who criticises others while he has all kinds of faults himself. "Why do you see the speck that is in your brother's eye, but do not notice the log that is in your own eye?" (Matthew 7:3). Here Jesus was drawing a picture of a man trying to take a speck of dust out of someone else's eye when he had a plank in his own eye! Locke, the great philosopher, called laughter "a sudden glory". If our Christianity does not make us happy it will not make us anything.

A Grateful Church

Verse 47 gives us still two more characteristics of that early Church. First, it describes the Christians as *praising God*. That is to say it was *a grateful Church*. There is so much, if we would only think of it, for which we ought to thank God. Our trouble is that we take so much for granted. We take things as if we had a perfect right to them and we forget that in reality they are gifts from God. Just because we always have them we forget what life would be like without them. There are three special things for which we ought to thank

God. First, we should thank God *for the world in which we live*. Once a man was staying in a highland cottage up in the hills. His host was not a wealthy man; he was a shepherd whose work took him out for long days and nights on to the hills. Every morning this man used to slip away out of the cottage on to the hillside and the man who was visiting the cottage used to wonder where he went. One day he asked him and the shepherd answered, "I go out every morning and I stand on the hillside and I take off my cap and thank God for the beauty of this world." We would do well to remember sometimes to give thanks to God for allowing us to live in a world like this. Second, we ought to give thanks *for ourselves*. One of the unfortunate things about life is that very often we do not appreciate a thing until we lose it. Health is like that and we would do well to thank God for bodies which are fit and healthy and minds that are sound and keen. Someone once wrote a little poem like this:—

> I did not realise what privilege to walk,
> Until a lame man limped along with sunshine in his talk.
> I did not realise what privilege to see,
> Until a blind man passed me by and seemed to smile
>   at me.
> I did not realise what privilege to hear,
> Until a deaf man spoke to me in words of hope and cheer.

Sometimes it would do us good if we were to think what life would be like if we could not walk or hear or see; that would make us give thanks to God that He has made us as we are. Third, and most of all, we should thank God *for Jesus*. God gave for men His only son and no one could give us a bigger or more wonderful gift than that.

If we will think of the world we live in, of ourselves and of our bodies and minds and of God's greatest gift of Jesus to us, we too will be praising God.

A Likeable Church

The description of the characteristics of the early Church

ends by telling us that the Christians had favour with all the people. That really means that *everybody liked them*. The early Christians made Christianity an attractive thing. There used to live in Scotland a famous minister called J. P. Struthers. He did the loveliest things and everyone loved him. He had a manse up on the hillside and the road the manse was on led out into the country and the young people who were courting used to walk along that road. Now Struthers was a gardener and he used to collect flowers from his garden and make them up into little posies and lay them on his garden wall; and the couples, as they passed by, knew that the flowers were for them and they used to take them and wear them. It was just a little thing, but it was a thing that not many people would have thought of, and it was the kind of thing that made everyone love Struthers. Our Christianity should make us so thoughtful and courteous and kind that everyone will like us and be glad to meet us. If religion turns a person into a hard, stern, unsympathetic person, always ready to criticise, to find fault and to condemn, that religion is not Christianity. Here is a good test. If a person is the kind of person from whom we would never dream of asking help, that person is not a Christian; but if a person is the kind of person to whom we would naturally go when we are in trouble that person has the spirit of Jesus. It is our duty to live such lovely lives that people will like us and will think well of the Master who made us like that.

The Characteristics of the Church

The people of the early Church were a *band of brothers*; our Christianity should make us friendly to one another. The early Christians were *happy folk*; a gloomy Christian is a contradiction in terms. The early Church was a *grateful Church*; if we will only make a deliberate effort every now and then to remember what God has done for us, we too will praise Him. The early Christians were *people whom everyone liked*; we too must live so finely that we will be good advertisements for Christianity.

QUESTIONS FOR DISCUSSION

1. What kind of things commonly cause trouble and quarrels within Churches and between Church members? Are they really important things?

2. Make out a list of things for which you want to thank God.

Chapter 4

THE COURAGE OF THE CHRISTIANS

In Acts, chapters 3 and 4 there is one of the great stories of courage in the history of the Christian Church. Peter and John had gone up to the Temple to pray. The beggars always sat at the Temple gates because they thought that they would find folk merciful and generous when they were on their way into the House of God. So by the Gate Beautiful there lay a man who all his life had been lame. He asked Peter and John for help as they passed in. They had no money to give him but they gave him far more—in the name of Jesus they gave him the health and the strength that he had never possessed and cured his lameness. A deed like that cannot be hidden and soon a great concourse of people came together. For Peter it was a tremendous opportunity and he preached to them of Jesus with power and with effect.

There was a Temple official called the Sagan; he was the man who was head of the Temple police and who was responsible for the good order of the Temple. When he saw this great crowd gathering he came down with his staff (Acts 4:1; he is called the captain of the Temple) and promptly arrested Peter and John. They were brought before the Sanhedrin. Consider the feelings of the Sanhedrin. Just rather more than seven weeks before they had tried Jesus, condemned Him and had arranged His crucifixion. They believed that once and for all they had eliminated this troublesome Jesus and that the whole episode was over. Think how they would feel when they discovered that the whole city was ringing with His name and when they saw His followers attracting crowds of people. No wonder they were angry.

To them Peter spoke with that dauntless courage which would never again deny its Lord. But the Sanhedrin was in a quandary. They could not deny that the man had been healed, for the man was there. They could not very well execute Peter and John for bringing health and healing to a lame man; there was no possible charge or crime there; so they compromised. They let them go but they laid down one condition—that they would never again preach or teach about Jesus. It was then that Peter and John made their great answer. "Whether it is right in the sight of God to listen to you rather than to God, you must judge; for we cannot but speak of what we have seen and heard" (Acts 4: 19, 20). And so they defied the Sanhedrin in the name of their Lord.

The Courage which knows

Theirs was the highest possible kind of courage; for it was the courage that knew perfectly well what must happen if they persisted in their chosen course. Peter and John knew that the very Sanhedrin before whom they stood had condemned Jesus and had arranged His death and that it could do the same to them.

There are two kinds of courage. There is the courage which recklessly dares to do a thing without knowing what the consequences will be. And there is the far greater courage which knows what the consequences must be and which, open-eyed, goes on. That is the courage which Peter and John possessed. And unless countless humble men and women had possessed that courage we would not have a Christian Church today. The martyrs in the early centuries knew what martyrdom meant. Often they had to stand by and see their own friends and their own nearest and dearest tortured and executed before their very eyes. They knew what was going to happen to them and yet they would not deny their Lord.

We will not today be martyred; but often we know quite well that if we do the right thing certain consequences must follow. Often it is hard to go on, knowing these things, but that is the highest kind of courage and that is the courage the Christian must have.

The Courage that will not be overawed

Further, Peter and John had a courage that would not be overawed. They were humble Galilean fishermen. They had no great education; they had no technical qualifications; they had no social standing; they were what the Sanhedrin contemptuously called "uneducated, common men" (Acts 4:13). The Sanhedrin had on it men with the highest academic and intellectual distinctions, men with the greatest wealth and the highest social standing. But Peter and John in face of that refused to be overawed. They did not care what men thought of them so long as they were true to Jesus.

In the days of the Reformation, Martin Luther was summoned to the town of Worms to answer for his faith. He was only a humble monk with no place or power or influence. He was told that if he went he would have to meet the greatest men in the Roman Catholic Church and that if they got him into their power it would go ill with him. He answered, "I would go to Worms if there were as many devils there as there are tiles on the housetops." He was told that if he went Duke George would oppose him and arrest him. "I would go," he said, "if it rained Duke Georges."

It may sometimes be that if we are going to be true to our Christian principles we will get up against quite important and sometimes very influential people. It might well be, for instance, that a man might have to choose between his Christian principles and getting up against his employer, or he might know that he could get a good and comfortable job if he were prepared to do certain things which were not quite right. At such times we must be like Peter and John and refuse to be overawed by anyone, however important.

The Courage that cannot be conquered

Still further, Peter and John displayed the courage that could not be conquered. It would have been easier to give in but they stood by their faith. If a man really stands by his faith and utterly refuses to move you can do nothing with him. He is the real conqueror. After a great battle between the English and the Dutch navies, in which the English took a terrific battering but would not admit defeat, De Witt, the Dutch leader, paid the English sailors a great tribute. "English sailors may be killed," he said, "but they cannot be conquered."

We must always remember that if we stand by our principles we may have to suffer for it; but even if we suffer we are the real conquerors because we have defied the worst that others can do to us and have refused to abandon our Master.

The Courage that comes from Certainty

Peter and John had this courage because they were quite sure they were right. "We cannot," they said, "but speak of what we have seen and heard" (Acts 4:20). They knew that they were right. It was not just a perhaps or a maybe on which they were staking everything. They knew what Jesus had done and could do, and because they knew they would not move. In the early days a Christian called Justin was brought before the Roman magistrate called Junius Rusticus. Justin would not abandon his faith in spite of every threat. Junius said to him, "Do you really suppose that you will ascend up to heaven and receive some recompense there?" "I do not suppose it," said Justin. "I know it and am persuaded of it."

It is only when we really know Jesus and when we really understand how right He is that we can be really brave. The best way to be brave and the best way to learn to take the stand we ought for Jesus is to know Him better every day.

The Courage which comes from God

But the real source of the courage of Peter and John was that they knew that they were doing the thing God wanted them to do. The Sanhedrin might be very learned and very powerful but the orders of the Sanhedrin were nothing as compared with the orders of God. After all, think of it this way. Any reward or punishment the Sanhedrin might inflict on them could last only while life lasted and that is not so very long; the prize of God would last for all eternity. It was better, far better, to be right with God and wrong with men, even if being right with God meant suffering for a season.

When Luther was given a chance to withdraw his statements and to recant he said, "Here I stand; I can do no other; so help me God." He felt that he could not do other than stand by God. In George Bernard Shaw's play there is a scene where Saint Joan knows that she has been abandoned by the men who should have been her supporters and that from now on she is alone. As she leaves them she turns and says, "I see now that the loneliness of God is His strength; what would He be if He listened to your jealous little counsels? Well, my loneliness shall be my strength too; it is better to be alone with God; His friendship will not fail me, nor His counsel, nor His Love. In His strength I will dare and dare and dare until I die." It is always better to be right with God. When we know that we are on God's side we may know that all kinds of things can happen to us, but we can also be sure that in the end it will be well.

Very often in this world, we will have to make a choice between doing what the world allows and avoiding trouble, and standing with God and principle and running into trouble. For the Christian there is really no choice. He knows that he must side with God.

In the end the strange thing is that it is not so difficult as it seems. In the sixteenth century, in England in the time of the martyrs, there was a man called Rogers, who had been a friend of Tyndale. He was condemned to death and he was burned at the stake. One who saw him die tells us that he died bathing his hands in the flame "as if it had been in cold water". We can be quite sure of this—that if we are given a hard task to do and if we have to come through a difficult time for the sake of what is right, God will help. It is the great thing about God that He can and does give to those who are true to Him strength to pass the breaking point and not to break.

The Courage of the Christians

When Peter and John stood before the Sanhedrin they

showed themselves men of courage. They showed the courage that knew what could happen but would not be deterred from that which was right. They showed the courage that refused to be overawed in any company. They showed the courage that refused to be defeated. Their courage came from their certainty that they were right. And the secret of their courage was God and the help which God gave them to be brave.

QUESTIONS FOR DISCUSSION

1. What kinds of temptations come to us to be false to our principles?

2. How can we be sure that we really are on God's side?

3. In what things should we be absolutely unyielding?

Chapter 5

THE FIRST OFFICE-BEARERS

In many ways it is true to say that the sixth chapter of the Book of Acts is one of the most interesting and suggestive chapters of the New Testament. It describes the appointment of the first set of office-bearers the Church ever had. Let us then begin by seeing how these men were appointed.

The early Church had its problems and it was out of these problems that this appointment took place. There were some practices which the Church took over from the Synagogue. One of the finest characteristics of the Jews was (and still is) an intense feeling of responsibility for their poorer brethren. No people have ever been so conscientious in remembering their duty to their own poor people. In the days of the early Church, the Synagogue had two closely related customs. Every Friday morning two official collectors went round the markets and the shops and the private houses and collected contributions both in cash and in food for the support of the poor. Later in the day other people went round and distributed this food and money to the poor. And every poor person was given enough food for fourteen meals, which was sufficient to keep him going for a week. The fund from which this distribution was made was called the *Kuppah*, which means the *basket*. In addition to this weekly collection and distribution there was also a daily collection from house to house taken from members of the Synagogue to meet sudden needs and sudden emergencies and to help those who were suddenly left destitute. This collection was called the *Tamhui*, which means the *tray*.

The Christian Church very wisely took this custom over but in the discharge of it certain difficulties arose. In Jerusalem at this time there were two kinds of Jews within the Christian Church. First, there were the Jews who had never left

Palestine and who spoke Aramaic, the language of Palestine. They are the people who are described in Acts 6:1 as Hebrews. Second, there were the Jews who had come from abroad. Many of them had lived for generations outside of Palestine. Very likely they had come up for the Passover or for Pentecost and during their visit they had become attached to the Christian Church, and their whole lives had been changed and they had decided never to go back to their homes again but always to stay in touch with the Church at Jerusalem. Many of these Jews from beyond Palestine had been away from Palestine for so many generations that they had actually forgotten their own language and spoke Greek instead of Aramaic. They are the people whom Acts 6:1 describes as Hellenists.

We know that the rigid, orthodox, strict Jews had a hatred and a contempt for all things foreign; and the Jews of Palestine to some extent looked down on these foreign Jews, rather as renegades from their native faith and traditions. Relations between the two sets of Jews were somewhat strained. So the charge arose that the *basket* and the *tray* were not being fairly distributed and that the widows of the Palestinian Jews were getting more than their share and the widows of the foreign Jews were not getting enough. The apostles were too occupied with preaching and teaching to hold an investigation into an argument like that and so they appointed seven men—their names are in Acts 6:5—to settle this matter and to see that practical justice was done. Often these men are called the Seven Deacons, but the word Deacon does not occur in this chapter. They were just seven men who were charged with the task of seeing that the poor were fairly treated and that the hungry had enough to eat.

Differing Gifts

Now this appointment is very interesting. For one thing it shows us that the Church needs amongst its officials men who have all kinds of gifts. The main gift of the apostles, of men like Peter and John, lay in preaching and teaching and instructing the people. The main gift of the Seven lay in practical administration of the affairs of the Christian Church. And the Church needed both kinds of gifts.

The Church needs both kinds of gifts even yet. When we use the phrase a *servant of God*, we usually think of a minister of the Church, or of someone who teaches in a Sunday School or Bible Class, or of someone who sings in a choir or can pray in public or who can address meetings. It is a very great pity that the words *servant of God* have been limited like that. The Church needs all kinds of gifts. No matter what kind of gift a man has the Church can use it. The Church needs its craftsmen as well as those who have the gift of speech.

In the old days when people needed a Church they built it themselves. The great cathedrals and the abbeys and the noble churches of the Middle Ages were built by the monks and the people. There is no reason why a Church should ever have to employ a tradesman to do any job that needs to be done. The carpenter, the electrician, the mason, the plumber, the plasterer, the painter, all kinds of craftsmen should be ready to lay their gifts at the service of the Church. It would be a great thing if that would happen because if we had an actual and literal hand in the constructing and the upkeeping of the Church it would become *our* Church, our personal possession, in a way that it never was before. Every one of us should say to ourselves, "Is there any job I can do in this Church?" and when we do it we should think of ourselves as having the great honour of being servants of God.

Actions not Words

Further, it is very important to notice that the first office-bearers to be appointed were men whose duty it was, not to sit round a table and talk, but to do a bit of practical service for their fellow-men. Here we see as clearly as can be that what God wants from us is not words, however fine, but deeds. He wants us, not to talk about things, but actually to get down to helping people.

Leslie Weatherhead in one of his books tells a story like this. There was a girl lying dying in a London hospital. She was quite young but she was literally tired to death. Her parents had died when she was very young and she was the eldest of the family and she had actually worked herself to death looking after her younger brothers and sisters. A visitor came to the hospital. The visitor was one of these hard people with no sense of what is kind and Christlike. The visitor said to this girl, "I suppose you know you're dying. What are you going to do when you go to stand before God?" The girl just did not know. The visitor went on. "Were you ever baptised?" No, the girl's parents had never thought of that. "Did you ever go to Sunday School or Church?" No, she had been too busy looking after her younger brothers and sisters for that. "Then," said this bullying visitor, "what are you going to do when you go to God?" For a moment or two the girl did not say anything; then she looked down at her hands lying on the white coverlet of the hospital bed. They were all rough and red and hacked with the work that she had had to do; and she said softly, "What am I going to do when I go to stand before God? I think I'll just show him my hands." There is no doubt these hands would be a passport for her to the glory of God because they had done so much for others. We must remember that God will not judge us by what we have said—anyone can produce fine words—God will judge us by what we have *done* for others.

Ready for any Task

But further, we see in this story of the first office-bearers that the members of the early Church were ready to turn their hands to any task. These seven men might well have said, "We want to preach and teach; we don't want this wretched job of seeing that food is distributed to hungry people." They might have turned up their noses at the job that was offered to them. But they did not. They must have said to themselves, "Here's a job some one has got to do; the Church wants me to do it; I'll take it on." What every Church needs is people who are prepared to do anything. It is always possible to get people to do jobs which get publicity and prestige and praise and thanks. It is not so easy to get people to do the thankless jobs which no one ever sees. We must look at it this way—any job in the Church is done for God and just because of that the humblest job can be clad with glory.

> Teach me, my God and King,
>   In all things Thee to see;
> And what I do in anything,
>   To do it as for Thee!
>
> All may of Thee partake;
>   Nothing can be so mean,
> Which with this tincture, "for Thy sake,"
>   Will not grow bright and clean.
>
> A servant with this clause
>   Makes drudgery divine:
> Who sweeps a room, as for Thy laws,
>   Makes that and the action fine.

Stepping Stones to Higher Things

There is one thing more about this story—it tells us that quite humble beginnings may well be the stepping stones to far greater things. At least two of these seven men became great figures in the Church. Stephen became one of the greatest of all the early Christian preachers and the first of the Christian martyrs (Acts 6:9-7:60). Philip became the man who deserves the title of the first of all the missionaries (Acts 8). They began with a humble job; they did that one so well that they moved on to a far bigger one.

Booker Washington was a Negro. He was one of the greatest men in the world and became Principal of Tuskegee University; but when he was young it was very difficult for a black man to get any education at all in the United States. He heard of a university which would accept coloured students and he walked hundreds of miles to get there. When he did get there he found that it was full up. They would not let him into the classes but they offered him a job sweeping the floors and making the beds. He took it and he swept floors so diligently and made beds so well that before long they took him as a student. He did a small job so well that in due time the bigger chance came to him.

We must learn that the only way to get onwards and upwards is to do what we have to do with all our might. Faithful service will always have its reward; and the reward of a small task well done will always be the chance of a bigger job to do.

The first Office-bearers

The appointment of these seven men as the first office-bearers of the Church shows us that the Church needs all kinds of gifts in her service. It shows us that it is not fine words but fine deeds which make a man a real servant of Christ. It shows us that the Church needs people who are ready to turn their hand to anything. And it shows us that the humblest job, if faithfully done, can lead to greater things.

QUESTIONS FOR DISCUSSION

1. Do you think that the Church uses the talents and the craftsmanship of its members as well and as fully as it might?

2. Think out some jobs that your friends and you yourself might do for your Church.

3. What would you say to someone who was discontented with his job?

Chapter 6

THE BROKEN BARRIERS

The tenth chapter of the Book of Acts describes what was perhaps the greatest turning-point in all the history of the Christian Church. Every devout Jew prayed three times a day. The Jewish day started at 6 a.m. and finished at 6 p.m. and the hours of prayer were the third, the sixth and the ninth hour, that is 9 a.m., 12 midday and 3 p.m. It was the midday time of prayer and Peter had gone to pray. Jewish houses usually had only one room and in a house like that with a large family in it, privacy was quite impossible; but Jewish houses had a flat roof, usually with an outside stair leading up to it. Round the roof there was a low parapet and often when a person wanted rest or quiet he went up to the roof top to be alone; so Peter went up to the roof top to pray.

There he saw a vision. He saw what looked like a great sheet let down from heaven and on the sheet was every kind of animal. The voice of God seemed to come to Peter telling him to kill and eat. But Peter was a devout Jew and to the devout Jew certain animals were unclean; it was considered a sin to eat them. (The whole list of unclean animals will be found in Leviticus 11.) So Peter was shocked by this commandment. "How can I do that?" he demanded. "I have never eaten anything that is common or unclean." Then the word of God came to Peter, "Never call any creature I have made common or unclean." This happened three times so that Peter could be in no doubt as to what God's message was.

A World of Barriers

Now we must ask, "Why did Peter need to have that vision sent to him?" He needed it because he lived in a world of barriers. He lived in a world where one half of the world despised the other half, and where men just had not the slightest idea that God could possibly want every man. Let us glance at some of these barriers to see what that ancient world was like.

(a) There was the barrier between *Jew and Gentile*. The Jews considered themselves the chosen people. They interpreted that to mean that God had no use for any other people but them. At best the Gentiles existed to be, some day, their slaves. At worst God had created Gentiles to be fuel for the fires of Hell. That God could want or love the Gentiles was something which they could not grasp.

(b) In the Jewish world there was the barrier between *men and women*. In the Jewish world women were despised. It was considered to be casting pearls before swine to educate a woman. No strict Jewish teacher would be seen talking to a woman on the street, not even to his own wife or mother or sister. In the form of prayer that a Jew used every morning there was a thanksgiving in which the Jew said, "I thank Thee, O God, that Thou has not made me a Gentile, a slave or a woman." Women were beyond the pale.

(c) In the Roman world there was the barrier between *the Roman and the non-Roman*. The Roman looked down on every other nation as lesser breeds. He had a contempt for other men and considered them fit only to be subjects for Roman rule.

(d) In the Greek world there were three barriers. There was the barrier between *the Greek and the non-Greek*. The Greek called the non-Greek a *barbarian*, literally a man who says *bar-bar*. The man who could not speak Greek was less than a man.

(e) There was the barrier between *the free man and the slave*. Aristotle, one of the greatest of all the Greek thinkers, held that civilisation was founded on slavery, that there were certain men fit only to be slaves, to exist to be the hewers of wood and the drawers of water for the cultured classes. It was quite wrong to educate these people or to try to lift them up. Slaves they were by nature and slaves they must remain.

(f) There was the barrier between *the ignorant man and the wise man.* Above the door of the Academy, the most famous Greek school of philosophy, there was the inscription, "Let no one ignorant of geometry enter here." The Greek teachers had no use for anyone who could not reach a certain intellectual standard. To them the simple and unlettered people did not matter.

There was nowhere in the ancient world where anyone could turn without coming up against these barriers which labelled all kinds of people common or unclean.

The Coming of Cornelius

Peter was a Jew and a devout Jew. Up to this time he had thought of the Jews as the chosen people and had never dreamed that God had any use for any other nation. Had he been told that God loved the Gentiles and wanted them he would certainly not have believed it. But this vision taught Peter that it was quite wrong to call any creature God had created common or unclean, and that above all it was quite wrong to think that there was any man whom God did not want. Immediately Peter's new discovery was put to the test. For word came to him at once that there were come to the house where he was staying emissaries from Cornelius, a certain Roman centurion who desired to become a Christian. An hour or two before, Peter would have slammed the door in his face and told him that God had no use for him; but now he knew better. So, as Acts 10 tells us, Cornelius was received into the Christian Church; and when Peter told the Christian brethren about it they were amazed and they glorified God saying, "Then to the Gentiles also God has granted repentance unto life" (Acts 11:18). This was one of the most, if not *the* most, important discoveries the early Church made. Had Peter not accepted and acted upon this vision, the Christian Church might have become simply a Jewish sect and *we* might never have been Christians at all.

Men of Every Race

From this story we learn certain great facts. First, we learn that God wants people of *every race*. There can be no racial distinctions in the Christian Church. Some years ago, a certain African Chief expressed his gratitude to King George the Sixth. He said, "Most white people speak to me as if I were a native; the King spoke to me as if I was another white man." Today, black people do not want to be considered either as inferior "natives" or as indistinguishable from white people. They are demanding that their dignity and worth as black people be recognised. We have a long way to go before we reach the ideal when we regard all men, whatever the colour of their skins, as equal in the sight of God and treat them as such. There are many parts of the United States where Negroes cannot get either education or housing as good as that available to whites. In South Africa there is a deliberate attempt to keep the natives down. In Great Britain distinguished non-white strangers can be refused entrance to hotels.

It is good to think of one's own nation as having a special place and a special destiny in the plan of God; but that place and destiny is not to lord it over other races but to bring to them the knowledge and the love of God. We can do a great deal in this direction by treating people of other nations as friends whenever we meet them.

Men of every Class

But further, God wants people of *every class*. There must be no class distinctions in the Church. The early Church was the only place where all classes of people could meet together. Normally the master would have no dealings with his slaves other than to see that they did their tasks and to punish them sorely if they did not do them. The Christian Church was the only place where people of every class could and did sit side by side. Once Paul wrote a letter to his friend Philemon. He wrote it because he was sending back to him a runaway slave called Onesimus. This Onesimus had turned up in Rome and had somehow made contact with Paul. He had become a Christian and now Paul was sending him back to his master. And as he sends Onesimus back to Philemon he writes to ask

Philemon to receive him back "No longer as a slave, but more than a slave, as a beloved brother" (Philemon 16).

So long as we think ourselves better than other people we are not Christians. Snobbishness is always an ugly thing but it is ugliest of all when it invades the Christian Church.

Good and Bad

Not only does God want men of every nation and of every class; He wants men of *every kind*. He wants good and bad alike. That was another thing the Jews could not see. They believed that the only kind of people God wanted was good people. Often we begin a Church service with some verses of a very well-known Psalm: "Who shall ascend the hill of the Lord? And who shall stand in his holy place? He who has clean hands and a pure heart, who does not lift up his soul to what is false and does not swear deceitfully" (Psalm 24:3, 4). If we will just think about that we will see that its effect is really to shut everyone out. That was the Jewish idea, not the Christian idea. The Jews had a saying, "There is joy in heaven over one sinner who is wiped out." They believed that all God wanted to do with bad people was to obliterate them. But Jesus came to teach us that God loves all men. He loves the good people with a love which makes Him glad and the bad people with a love which makes Him sad; and He sent His Son to make bad men good.

We must remember that in the last analysis we have no right to think ourselves better than anyone else; and we must remember that we must never look down on anyone. Contempt is one of the worst of all sins because God wants all men alike.

Nothing common or unclean

Peter had to learn the lesson that all men are dear to God. In the Church there must be no racial distinctions; there must be no class distinctions; there must be no contempt for any man however far he may have fallen. To us also there must be no man who is common or unclean.

QUESTIONS FOR DISCUSSION

1. What can we do to eliminate racial distinctions?

2. Do you think that class distinctions still exist within the Church?

3. Suppose there came to a Church service, a person who was in the eyes of the Church a bad person, for instance a person who had served a prison sentence, or who had committed some grave moral fault—what kind of welcome do you think he or she would receive? How ought we to treat such a person?

PART 2: GOD'S CHALLENGE

Chapter 7

BE A GOOD SOLDIER OF JESUS CHRIST

When Paul was writing to his young friend Timothy, he gave him some good advice. He told him what he must do and what he must be if he was really to live the Christian life and serve the Christian Church. And one of the great things that he said to him was "Take your share of suffering as a good soldier of Christ Jesus" (2 Timothy 2:3). This title, "A soldier of Christ," is one of the titles of the Christian that we know best of all. It is one that comes into many of our hymns—"Onward, Christian soldiers," "Soldiers of Christ! arise," "Stand up! Stand up for Jesus, ye soldiers of the Cross". So, then, since we sing about it so often and talk about it so often, it is only right that we should think about what this title really means and about what a soldier of Christ should really be like. Let us look at the qualities which are the marks of a good soldier.

The Soldier's Obedience

The very first quality of the good soldier must be the quality of *obedience*. A soldier is first and foremost a man under orders. All the drill and the discipline that a soldier receives when he is under training is designed to one end. It is designed to make him such that at any time, and especially in some emergency, he will automatically obey the word of command. Obedience is not an easy virtue to win. Most of us, if we were honest, would have to admit that in our heart of hearts our ambition is to do what we like. The good soldier never does what he likes; he does what his commander tells him to do. We should be that way with Jesus. Our question should never be, "What do I want to do?" but "What does Jesus want me to do?"

One of the things that greatly helps obedience is if the person who gives the order is prepared to carry it out himself. Obedience is very difficult if someone gives us an order and then stands back and watches us do all the hard work; it is much easier if the leader shows that he is ready and willing to carry out his own orders. Nelson was one of the greatest of all English admirals and his sailors loved him. When he himself was quite a young officer he would see little midshipmen come aboard. The boys would be ordered to climb up to the masthead and he would see them looking fearfully at the high mast and the rigging, terrified to go aloft. When Nelson saw a lad like that he would challenge him to a race to the masthead. When at last they faced each other breathless at the peak, he would laugh at landlubbers ashore who were afraid of this kind of life and the boy would forget to be afraid. Nelson showed that he was quite ready to carry out his own orders. Now that is one of the great reasons why we should find it easier to carry out God's commands. God never orders us to do anything that He was not prepared to do Himself. It is not as if God sat peaceful in heaven and gave us His commands and looked down and watched us sweating it out. In Jesus, God came to this world, and lived this life, and faced our temptations and our difficulties and our work. The Christian soldier must first and foremost be obedient, but his obedience is given to a commander who never asked another to do what He was not prepared to do Himself.

The Soldier's Courage

For another thing, the good soldier must be *brave*. We must always remember that being brave does not mean never being afraid. It is easy to do a thing if we have no fear to do it. But real courage, the highest courage, is when we are desperately afraid to do something which is the right thing, and when we do it just the same. It is not fear that we should be ashamed of; what we should be ashamed of is allowing fear to stop us doing what we know to be right.

There is a vast difference between being *brave* and being

reckless, between being *courageous* and being *foolhardy*. Someone has very wisely put it this way: "The distinction between
courage and foolhardiness lies in knowing what dangers to
choose". It is not brave to risk taking a drink; it is not brave
to risk your money gambling; it is not brave to take some risk
which is going to involve others in risk to rescue you if anything
happens to go wrong; it is not brave to risk doing some
dishonourable thing in the hope of getting away with it.
These things are not brave; they are reckless and foolish.
But it is brave to take a risk to do the right thing, to know
that the straight and the honourable thing may get us into
trouble and make us unpopular and yet to do it. It is brave
in any circumstances to show what side we are on. In World
War I, the Gurkhas were fighting in the Middle East. A
little band of Gurkhas was sent out on a patrol. They never
came back and some people were suspicious that they had
gone over to the Turks. But then news came through and
this is what had happened. The Gurkhas had been cap-
tured by the Turks. They had been lined up and they had
been told that they must choose between joining the Turks
and being shot there and then. The officer in charge looked
at his little group of fellow Gurkhas and smiled. He took off
his cap and waved it in the air and said: "Three cheers for
King George!" Before the cheers had died away the sound
of the Turkish shots rang out and the Gurkhas dropped dead.
That was real courage because they had the courage to show
what side they were on, even if to show it meant death.

We must always be brave enough to do the right thing
and to show what side we are on if we are going to be good
soldiers of Christ.

The Soldier's Endurance

Still further, the good soldier must have the quality of
endurance. Someone has said that the test of a soldier is,
how does he fight when he is tired and hungry? It is easy to
keep going when things are going well: the real test is if we
can keep going when we are up against it. It is easy to play

when the team is winning; the real test is if we can play just as hard when the team is losing and when victory seems impossible.

During World War II, two battalions of the Coldstreams were caught and besieged in Tobruk. They fought their way out and when they got out, of two thousand men only two hundred were left alive; and they had had such a terrible time that they were only shadows of men. They were cared for by the R.A.F. when they reached an Air Force station. Some of the officers were talking in the R.A.F. mess and someone said to a major of the Coldstream Guards who had survived: "After all, as footguards, you had no option but to have a go". Another R.A.F. officer who was standing by said thoughtfully: "It must be pretty tough to be in the Brigade of Guards because your tradition compels you to carry on irrespective of circumstances". The Guards must never give in and never surrender. No matter what they are up against they must carry on. A Christian soldier must be like that. In World War I the Allied commander was Marshal Foch. He was once giving an officer instructions as he went into action. "You must not retire," said Foch. "You must hold on at all costs." "But," said the officer aghast, "that means we must all die." "Precisely!" answered Foch. One of the greatest of all tests of a soldier is just this ability to stick it out.

And that is the test of the Christian soldier. Life is not a sprint but a marathon race. It is not a quick dash and then over; it is something that we have to keep pegging away at all the time. In fact, life is often more like an obstacle race than even a marathon race and our job is to find a way past all the obstacles which meet us. It is just this ability to endure things, to face up to difficulties, to surmount obstacles, which makes the difference between a real man and a poor creature. A certain Viennese surgeon tells how two men came to him on the same day to have the same operation. Both had to have their right arm amputated at the shoulder. Both operations were successfully carried out, and two years later both men visited him in Vienna. The first man said,

"Doctor, I am helpless without my right arm; I cannot work; marriage is impossible to me; I am a log of wood, not a man at all." The second man said, "Doctor, I find I can get on beautifully without my right arm. I have a better job than before I lost it. I am married and I have a fine boy. I sometimes ask myself why nature provided us with two arms when one is quite enough!" There was all the difference in the world between these two men. The one lay down to his trouble and whined and whimpered about it and let it beat him. The other endured it and faced it and conquered it.

We have no right to expect life always to be easy. It is not always sunny weather and the wind is not always in our favour. If we are going to be good soldiers of Christ we need to have the endurance which will never lie down to things and which will never give in.

The Soldier's Sacrifice

And for one last thing, the good soldier is the man who is *prepared to lay down his life for his friend.* In wartime a soldier is not a soldier for his own sake. He is a soldier in order to protect his country and those whom he loves. He is not in the job for anything that he can get out of it; he is in the job for the sake of others. A famous Scottish minister tells how he was a chaplain in World War I. He had just arrived in France and he was going up the line for the first time. Suddenly he saw the body of a dead soldier, a kilted lad from a Highland regiment. And, when he saw it, there flashed into his mind a text, a thing that Jesus said: "This is my body, broken for you."

There are two ways of life. We can live life with no thought except the thought of what we are going to get out of it, of how we can be happy and comfortable and of how we can make things easy for ourselves. Or we can live life always thinking of what we can do for others, always thinking of how we can serve others, always thinking of what we can give and not of what we can get, always thinking of what we can put into life and not of what we can get out of it. There is no doubt about how the Christian ought to live. Our pattern and example is Jesus. "All the joy and the glory of heaven was his by right, but he became a man and a servant and was obedient unto death, even the death of the Cross" (Philippians 2:5-8). We, too, must be like that.

The Christian soldier must think, not of what he can get for himself, but of what he can do for others.

A Good Soldier of Christ

One of the greatest titles of the Christian is a good soldier of Jesus Christ. A good soldier must be *obedient*. We must always obey God and we must always remember that God never asks us to do what He was not prepared to do Himself. A good soldier must be *brave*. We must never recklessly risk doing things which are dangerous and wrong; but we must always be brave enough to do the right thing and to show where we stand. A good soldier must be *enduring*. We must be able to keep on when everything is against us. A good soldier must be *ready to sacrifice his life for his friends*. We, too, must be ready to spend ourselves for others, because that is what Jesus did and we must follow in His steps.

QUESTIONS FOR DISCUSSION

1. In what kind of things do we tend to disobey God?

2. What chances do we get to show what side we are on?

3. What kind of difficulties may we have to face?

4. In what ways can we live selfishly? In what ways can we serve others?

Chapter 8

BE A PILGRIM

In the ancient world the pilgrim was a very common figure. Long ago people would scrape and save for years to visit some place which they regarded as specially holy. People would journey half way across the world to see places like that; and these people were called *pilgrims*. The Jews were like that. The Jews were scattered all over the world, but every Jew had one great ambition—to eat one Passover in Jerusalem before he died; and so at the Passover time you would see Jews converging from all over the world on Jerusalem. To this day when Jews are celebrating the Passover in this and in other countries they finish the service with a prayer which thanks God that He has enabled them to eat the Passover here this year, and which prays that next year they may eat it in Jerusalem. In the Book of Psalms there is a very interesting set of Psalms. You will see that Psalms 120 to 134 all have the title "A Song of Ascents". Sometimes these are called the *Pilgrim Psalms*, and these are the psalms that the Jewish pilgrims sang to lighten the road on the long trek to Jerusalem. Every Mohammedan has the ambition to visit Mecca where Mohamet, the founder of their faith, was born. And when they have visited it they are entitled to wear a green fez which is the sign of a pilgrim who has been to Mecca. In the old days every Christian used to have the ambition to visit Jerusalem. Sometimes, in the centuries when people had to walk because there was no other way of getting there, Christians would spend years on a pilgrimage to Jerusalem, the city where Jesus walked and talked and died. In Great Britain, Canterbury was the great centre for pilgrims for that is the place in which Christianity first came to England.

A Man on the Way

What are the characteristics of the pilgrim? By far the

most outstanding thing is that a pilgrim is a man who is *always on the way*. He is going somewhere and he knows where he is going and every day in life he presses on to that goal. A pilgrim, when he pitched his camp for the night, would ask, How much farther on am I today? How much nearer have I got to my goal? The pilgrim is a man on the way. We should be like that. We should always be going somewhere.

There are three things in which we ought always to be pilgrims. (*a*) We should be pilgrims in *learning*. Every night we should sit down and ask ourselves, Is there anything I know tonight that I did not know this morning? Take the case of learning a language, say Latin or French or German. If we learned only ten new words a day, at the end of a year we would know 3,650 words and that is a vocabulary big enough to be sufficient for any language. And we should go on learning all our lives. The trouble is that so many people, when they leave school or when they pass their examinations, say to themselves, "Well, that's me finished with study and learning." That is precisely why they do not get on any further than they do. Cato learned Greek when he was eighty. When Mozart was already famous he took lessons in counterpoint. If we are going to make our mark in life we have to be pilgrims in learning, always adding something to our knowledge every day.

(*b*) We should be pilgrims in *goodness*. We ought to ask ourselves every day, Have I lived better today than I did yesterday? Have I got rid of some of the faults which spoil life for myself and for others? Have I succeeded in acquiring some new virtue which will make me kinder and more useful and more helpful? The trouble with most of us today is that we never really get any further on. We are quite content to remain the way we are. Paul said of himself, "One thing I do, forgetting what lies behind and straining forward to what lies ahead, I press on toward the goal" (Philippians 3:13, 14). The hymn speaks about

> Leaving every day behind
> Something which might hinder;

Running swifter every day,
Growing purer, kinder.

If we are going to live the Christian life we must be pilgrims in goodness.

(c) We should be pilgrims in *service*. There are two ideas about what constitutes success in life. Some people think that success means getting more and more done for us, controlling more and more people, getting more and more of our own way. Other people think that success means doing more and more for others, fitting ourselves every day to be better servants of others, not ruling others, but serving others. It is a good rule to look back on each day and to ask ourselves, Have I done anything for anyone today? And if the day has been spent entirely selfishly, then it is a wasted day. If we are to live the Christian life we must be pilgrims in service.

A Man who is not settled in the World

For another thing, the pilgrim is a man who has not settled down comfortably in one place, but who is always on the move to his goal which is ahead. The New Testament often uses a very interesting word about the Christian. It says that the Christian is a stranger in this world, or a *sojourner*. The word in Greek describes a visitor as opposed to a permanent resident. Now Christianity teaches us one thing very definitely. It teaches us that this world is not our permanent residence, but that we are on the way through it to another world. There is a saying of Jesus which is not in any of our gospels but which was discovered in an inscription: "This world is a bridge; the wise man will pass over it, but he will not build his house upon it". That does not mean that this world is quite unimportant and that we can despise it. It means the very reverse of that. In school and at our trade and everywhere else, we have faithfully to fulfil the duties and the tasks of one class before we are allowed on to the next; and this world is like a preparation class, a training school, a testing ground for the world to come. But it does mean this—that we must never get so occupied and immersed in this world that we forget altogether that there is another world to come. If we are really Christian we must be like the pilgrim who always sees his goal before him and who knows that he must faithfully discharge the duties of this stage before he can go on to the next.

A Man who travels Light

Still further, the pilgrim is *a man who travels light*. In the old days a pilgrim could not take a train or a bus or a motor car. He had to walk and just because of that he could not carry very much. So he had to think carefully what he was going to carry with him and he had to put aside everything that was not necessary and confine himself to the things which were absolutely essential. One of the most important things in life is to decide what is essential and to stick to that. If we go off on side lines and by-roads we waste our time and waste our energy. For instance, when we are at school and when we are learning our trade, it is essential to pass our examinations. Other things may be very interesting and very pleasant, but if we spend our time on them we have not time enough for what is essential, and we will be sorry for it when the day of the examination comes.

H. M. Stanley tells us what happened to him when he was journeying on foot across Africa. He started out with a convoy of native bearers and with a great deal of luggage and baggage. He took a lot of books to pass the time in the long delays and in the necessary encampments. One by one his native carriers fell ill or died or deserted until he was left with very few. The unessential things had to be flung away. He tells us that when he got to the other side of Africa, he had only two books left—a one-volume edition of Shakespeare's plays and the Bible; and he said that if Africa had been any wider Shakespeare would have had to go, too. The Bible was the essential book.

We soon discover that in this world we cannot do everything and we have to concentrate on the things that are essential or we do not get anywhere at all. There are three parts of us. We have a *body*. It is essential to train that body to keep it

fit and healthy. That is one thing we must always find time
for, otherwise we will not be able to do our work at all. We
have a *mind*. It is essential to store and train that mind.
Games and amusements and pleasures and relaxations are all
necessary and all interesting and all a part of life, but they
must never encroach on the time that should be spent in work
and in study. We have a *spirit*. The spirit is the part of us
that lives on even when our body dies. It is therefore obviously
the most important part of all; and if we train our bodies and
store our minds and forget that we have a spirit we are neglect-
ing the most important part. The essential things are the
things which keep our bodies fit, our minds keen and which
enable us to know God better every day.

A Man who sticks to the Road

And for one last thing, the pilgrim is *a man who sticks to the
road*. If we are just out for a country walk it does not matter
how many side roads we follow or how many byways we
explore; but if we are out to go somewhere, we have to stick
to the main road in order not to waste time and to get there
as soon as possible. That is the difference between a pilgrim
and a man who is out for a stroll. Now there is one way and
one way only to stick to the main road of life. Jesus said,
"I am the way" (John 14:6). A great New Testament writer
urged us to run, "looking to Jesus" (Hebrews 12:2). If we
want to stick to the main road of life, we must walk it always
looking to Jesus, more—always with Jesus. If we stick to
Him, we will never stray down the by-roads on which we
might get lost.

The Christian Pilgrim

The true Christian is to be a pilgrim. A pilgrim is a man
who is always on the way. We must be pilgrims in learning,
pilgrims in ·goodness, pilgrims in service, growing wiser,
and purer and kinder every day. The pilgrim is a man who
knows that he must not settle down comfortably in one place.
We must remember that we are on the way to another world,
and what happens to us there will depend on how we use

this world. The pilgrim is a man who travels light. We must be quite sure of what is essential in life and we must concentrate on that. The pilgrim is a man who sticks to the road. We will only succeed in never straying from the right way when we walk with Jesus all the way.

QUESTIONS FOR DISCUSSION

1. How can we find time for the self-examination which is necessary if we are to be sure we are always on the way?

2. How can we remind ourselves that this world is a bridge to the other world?

3. What are the really essential things in life?

4. What are the by-roads down which we may stray if we try to walk alone?

Chapter 9

BE A LIGHT OF THE WORLD

When Jesus was talking to His men, He said to them, "You are the light of the world" (Matthew 5:14). When Paul was writing to his friends in Philippi and when he was thinking of them trying to live out the Christian life in a heathen and a pagan city, he said to them, "You shine as lights in the world" (Philippians 2:15). So, then, it is clear that the New Testament says that the person who is trying to be a Christian must be like a light in the world. Let us see if we can find out what that means for us.

A Light which can be Seen

The first thing which strikes anyone about a light is that *a light can be seen*. After Jesus had said that His friends must be the lights of the world, He went on to say that a city that is on a hill cannot be hidden. A city that stands on a hilltop strikes the eye straight away. We can see it miles away. It stands out from the surrounding countryside so that everyone can see it. A light is like that. On a dark night you can see a candle or even a match being struck a long distance away. So, then, first and foremost, when Jesus said that we must be the lights of the world, He meant that we must make our Christianity to be seen. Sometimes that is by no means easy. It is very natural to wish not to be different from other people. The easy way to live is simply to do what others do and act as others act. But the Christian must stand out from other people.

There are at least three ways in which a Christian ought to be different from others. (1) He ought to be *braver than other people*. General Gordon was a great Christian soldier. When he was in China he used to walk about, armed with nothing but a cane, in the most dangerous circumstances.

Once when he was coolly walking about when things were really dangerous, one of his soldiers said, "Gordon's never afraid. He's one of these Christians." The real reason why a Christian is brave is that he knows that he is never alone because Jesus is always with him, and he knows that no matter what happens to him, in life or in death, it cannot separate him from Jesus.

In World War II there was a lad called John Pennington. He was only twenty years of age and he joined the R.A.F. Before he became an airman he had been a choirboy for many years. He was the pilot of a four-engined Lancaster bomber. They were hedge-hopping over France one night when fire developed in the port engine. The flight-engineer seemed to have got the fire stopped and they flew on, on three engines. Then the fire started again and things looked very grim. John Pennington said to himself, "We're in a spot." And then he began to speak into the inter-communication radio and this is what he was saying: "Lighten our darkness, we beseech Thee, O Lord, and by Thy great mercy defend us from the perils and dangers of this night. Amen." And all the crew echoed that "Amen". It was the prayer that he had so often joined in at evening worship. And it gave him and his friends their courage back again that night because it made them remember that Jesus was with them. It will help us to be brave if we think about Jesus who is always with us.

(2) The Christian ought to be *happier than other people*. There are still people who have the idea that Christianity is a gloomy thing. When Jesus walked this earth, the criticism of Him was that He was far too happy. They said that He was a "glutton and a drunkard, a friend of tax collectors and sinners!" (Matthew 11:19). He was obviously the kind of person who enjoyed life. It is a very notable thing how often Jesus told stories about weddings and feasts. In Luke 14:7-24 He told a whole series of stories about feasts. To Him to be in the Kingdom of God was to be as happy as if He were sitting at a wedding feast.

A pupil once said of a great Christian teacher, "She made me feel as if I were bathed in sunshine." After all, the word

Gospel literally means *good news*. A Christian is a man who has received good news of God. He has discovered how much God loves him, and how all the time God is watching over him, and that ought to make him always happy. Once there was a little girl in a hospital ward. Christmas time came round and a minister came into the ward to tell the Christmas story. The little girl had never heard it before. After the service was over, she said to one of the nurses, "Did you ever hear that story about Jesus before?" "Of course," said the nurse, "I've often heard it before." "Well, then," said the little girl, "you don't look as if you had." The Christian is the person who has heard the good news, and the good news should make him happy.

(3) The Christian ought to be more *honourable* than other people. Tommy Walker was a very famous Scottish international football player. If World War II had not intervened he might well have been a minister of the Church. He was a really Christian man. When he was playing in the Scottish League, a famous referee said of him: "When I referee a match where Tommy Walker is playing, I know that I have only twenty-one players to watch, not twenty-two, because Tommy would never do a dirty thing".

Because he was a Christian he was a fairer and cleaner football player. To be a Christian is not merely something which has to do with going to Church. It means being a more diligent scholar, a better workman, a more conscientious tradesman, a cleaner and more honourable games player than the person who is not a Christian. It should be just as possible to recognise a Christian at work, in school or on the playing fields, as it is in Church. When Jesus said that we must be lights of the world, He meant that our Christianity must be plain for all to see.

A Light which Guides

Another thing that is characteristic of a light is that *a light guides people*. Some of us can remember how very difficult it was to find one's way about in the black-out during World

War II when there was no street lighting. If you travel by Underground in London the way to different places is indicated by different coloured lights and all you have to do to find a train for the place to which you want to go is to follow a light of a certain colour. If you live near a river where there is shipping, and you go out and stand on the river bank when it is dark, you will see right down the river the long line of lights which show the steersman the channel along which the ship must sail if she is to voyage safely. When there is a dangerous bit of coast or where there is a reef or a rock which might wreck a ship, a lighthouse is put up to show the ship the right way in which to go. A light is often the thing that shows us where to go and keeps us from getting lost. The Christian must be a light like that. That is to say, the Christian must be an example to others to show them the right way and to help them to keep to it.

There is nothing like the power of a great example. Dunkirk was one of the great episodes of World War II. The troops of the allied armies were driven right to the sea coast of the continent. The great majority of them were rescued, by being brought to this country in every kind of boat that was able to sail and to stay afloat. When they got to this country, they had lost their equipment and many of them had lost heart, too. But there was one regiment which never lost heart and never lowered its standards and that regiment was the Guards. On the beaches at Dunkirk, when they were being bombed and when life was in danger, they actually held a kit inspection.

Towards the end of the evacuation there was a number of French soldiers in one of our English ports. They had been brought safely across the Channel; but they had lost everything. They had lost their equipment and, what was worse, they had even lost their country. They were lying on the quay utterly weary and dispirited and listless. They had given up trying. Then off one of the ships marched the Guards. Even though they had come from Dunkirk, they were shaved and tidy and their equipment was intact and they marched off the pier as if they were changing the guard at Buckingham Palace.

One of the Frenchmen looked up. At first in his eyes there was utter amazement. Then he got to his feet, squared his shoulders, fell in behind the Guards and marched on, and all his fellow countrymen who were there did the same. The example of the Guards had changed them from dull, dispirited, defeated men into self-respecting soldiers once again. A great example gave them back their courage and their hope and their heart.

In this world it is true to say that a great many people are only waiting for a good example. If someone will only give them a lead they will do the right thing and follow the right course. They have not got the courage and the strength to make their own decisions. Left to themselves they will take the easy way and follow the crowd; but if someone gives them an example and a lead they will do the right thing. We have to be that example.

Peter said a fine thing about Jesus. He said that Jesus left us "an example, that you should follow in His steps" (1 Peter 2:21). The word he uses in the Greek for *example* is very interesting. It is the word that is used for the line of copper-plate writing at the top of the page of a writing exercise book. In an exercise book like that there is at the top of the page a line of perfect writing and we learn to write by copying the example. Jesus left us an example, and, if we follow that example, we in turn will be an example to others. There is always someone who is watching us, a friend, or a younger person; and that person may follow the example we give. It is a great responsibility that is laid upon us. We have to be lights of the world showing people where the right way is and helping them to walk in it and to keep to it. We, in our lives, our words, our conduct, have to pass on to others the example of Jesus Himself.

A Light which Warns

There is one other kind of light—there is the light which warns. If there is a dangerous obstruction on the road, there will be a red light there to warn the traveller to beware. If the engine driver sees the signal at red he knows to stop, and if the motorist sees the traffic lights at red he will halt, for to go on would be to risk an accident. On level-crossing gates, on an opening bridge or a swing bridge, before you come to a ferry or a river, there will be a red light to warn that it is dangerous to proceed. The light warns about danger and saves from danger. That is one of the tasks of the Christian—to warn others who are running into danger and to save them from making mistakes. Often a word of warning spoken in time will save a person from a great deal of trouble later on. If we see a friend or an acquaintance following a course which can only lead to trouble it is our duty to speak that word of warning which will stop him. It is not a question of speaking it in anger, or in criticism, or in a fault-finding way. It is a question of speaking it in a kindly and a very friendly way. If we keep another from doing wrong we will have done something well worth while.

Lights of the World

If we are going to be lights of the world we ourselves must always follow Him Who is The Light of the World. We can never show others what to do unless Jesus shows *us* what to do. But when we know Jesus and so know what is right, we have a duty to help others to do the right. We have to live in such a way that people will see that we are Christians. We have to show them how brave, how happy, how honourable a Christian can be. We have to be a good example to others, because there are very many people who are only waiting for an example and for a lead. We have to speak a word of warning to others when we see them doing things which can only lead to harm and trouble. If we do these things we, too, will obey Jesus' commandment to be lights of the world.

QUESTIONS FOR DISCUSSION

1. What opportunities do we get to show others that we belong to Jesus and that we are trying to follow the Christian way?

2. What are the kinds of things in which we can be an example to others? In what kind of things can we give a lead to others who have not the strength of will and purpose to do the right thing themselves?

3. What kind of things should we warn others against? How can we warn others in such a way that they will accept the warning and not resent it?

Chapter 10

BE GOD'S FELLOW-WORKER

One of the greatest honours and privileges that a man can have is to help some great man in some great work. When we were very young it used to be a great thrill to help our mothers and we felt very important when we were allowed to do so. If we knew that some great man was engaged in some great project to bring help and healing to a great many people, it would be a very real honour and a very real privilege to be allowed to be his assistant. Now Paul once took to himself and gave to other Christians a title which is the greatest title that a Christian can have. He said we are *fellow-workers for God* (1 Corinthians 3:9). That is to say, we are God's helpers, God's assistants, God's fellow-labourers and surely there could be no greater honour than that.

Doing things with God

One of the great facts of the Christian life is this—that it is true to say, in one sense, that God is just as helpless without us as we are without God. God very seldom acts directly in this world. If God wants something done He has to get a man or a woman to do it for Him. For instance, if God wants a child taught, He has to get a teacher to teach him. If God wants a sick person healed, He has got to get a physician or a surgeon to bring to that person His healing power. God needs His fellow-workers.

Dick Sheppard, a famous minister and preacher, used to have a story which he loved to tell. There was a man who had an allotment. When he got it, it was absolutely waste ground, filled with weeds and wild grass and covered with stones and bits of rock. He worked and worked at it until he made it a lovely place which grew the finest vegetables and the loveliest flowers. Once he was showing a very pious friend round his allotment and letting him see his vegetables and his flowers. "Yes," said the friend, "it's wonderful what God can make grow on a bit of ground." "Yes," said the man, "but you should have seen this bit of ground when God had it to Himself." The ground could never have been cleaned and enriched and fertilised; the vegetables and the flowers could never have grown, unless the man who sweated and dug and toiled and thought, had been prepared to be God's fellow-labourer, to work with God.

That is what Paul meant when he described the Church as *The Body of Christ*. Christ is no longer here in the body; He is here in the spirit. So if He wants something done He has got to get one of us to do it for Him. If He wants a sad person comforted, a lonely person visited, a hard-pressed person helped, He must find someone to do it for him. Quite literally we have to be hands to work for Jesus, feet to run upon His errands, a voice to speak for Him. We have to be the body through which He works; we have to be His fellow-labourers. It is one of our greatest privileges, one of the most thrilling things in life, to think that we can be the helpers, the fellow-workers of God.

Helping to win Others

For one thing, He needs our help to bring others to Him and to tell others about Him. When Paul is thinking about the people who are not yet Christians, he says, "How are they to believe in him of whom they have never heard? And how are they to hear without a preacher?" (Romans 10:14). How can people ever hear about Jesus unless someone tells them about Him? The people in heathen lands could never hear about Jesus unless the missionary went to tell them the story of Him. We, too, can share in this. We do not need to preach; we do not need to talk about Jesus. What we can do is this—we can bring someone to Church along with us. If we do that we are giving someone else the opportunity to hear about Jesus and about the kind of life that Jesus offers to us. We are really telling someone else about Jesus.

A famous Scottish preacher put it this way. Sometimes

when we are making a telephone call there is some difficulty in getting through to the person with whom we wish to get into touch. When that happens the operator will very likely say, "I'm trying to connect you," and when she has connected us she fades out and leaves us to talk to the person to whom we wish to talk. We have got the chance to be the operator who connects people with Jesus. If we enjoy a thing and if we think that it does us good, then surely the first thing that we should want to do is to share it with others, to give them a chance to benefit from the thing which has helped us. We should feel like that about the Church and about Jesus. And if we bring someone else along with us we are really telling the person about Jesus, because we are giving him a chance to hear about Jesus. And if we do that we are being fellow-workers with God.

Helping Others to understand

For another thing, God needs our help to show people what being a Christian means. He needs us to help others to understand what Christianity and the Christian life are. There is not really much use in talking to people about being a Christian; but there is all the use in the world in showing people how a Christian lives and what a Christian is.

When Philip met the Ethiopian on the road down to Gaza he heard the Ethiopian reading Isaiah 53. He heard because in those days people had hardly discovered at all how to read to themselves quietly; they always read aloud. He said to the Ethiopian, "Do you understand what you are reading?" The Ethiopian answered, "How can I, unless someone guides me?" (Acts 8:26-31). He needed someone to help him understand what being a Christian meant.

If a firm wants people to buy its products, what it often does is this. It hires a room and fills the room with the things it makes; and invites people to come and see them. Now that is what Jesus wants us to do. He wants us to be His products so that other people can see in us what being a Christian means.

H. L. Gee tells of an experience that he himself had.

During World War II he was staying on a farm. The farmer and his wife were called John and Mary. They lived very lovely Christian lives. On the farm there was a land girl. She was a very modern young person and when she came first she had no use at all for the Church or for Christianity. She was not interested at all in religion; in fact, she rather despised it. But the way that John and Mary lived compelled her to see that there *must* be something in a religion which produced people as fine as they were. When H. L. Gee was leaving the farm she was telling him how she had come to see that there was something in being a Christian after all, and she said something like this: "I find it hard to read the Bible because it is difficult to understand. I find it hard to pray for no one ever taught me how to. But I'm not worrying, because I know I'll find God by following Mary."

It is our job, not to talk about Jesus—anyone can do that—but in our own lives to try to show what Jesus is like. And that does not apply only to the times when we are in Church or on the Church premises. At home, at school, at work, on the playing fields, we have to let people see in our lives what Christianity is. If we do that, we will, in the best way, be explaining what Christianity is and we will be acting as fellow-workers with God.

Helping God by helping Others

For still another thing, God needs us to help others. God is sad when he sees any of his people sad. God wants something done when He sees any of His people up against it. God cares when he sees people who are poor and who have not enough, who are struggling with some task that is too much for them, who are lonely and friendless, who are carrying burdens that are very heavy. And the only way in which God can help these people is to get one of us to help them. When we do help others in any way we are helping God; we are being His fellow-workers.

Saint Christopher is supposed to be the saint who helps travellers and a legend tells how Saint Christopher got his name. A boy was born and his parents called him Opherus, a name which derives from a Greek word which means *to carry*; you might say it meant *the burden-bearer*. Opherus grew up to be exceptionally tall and strong; he was a young giant. He made up his mind that he would give his life only to the strongest and to the best. First he took service with a king. But he discovered that this king was terrified of the devil. You had only to mention the devil's name to make him tremble. So, because the devil seemed so strong, Opherus took service with Satan. But he discovered that Satan trembled whenever he saw a cross, and so Opherus determined to find out what the cross stood for. He found an old monk called Babylas and Babylas told him all about Jesus. So Opherus determined to serve Jesus, but he did not quite know how to do this. Near the monk's cell there was a river which ran very fast and high, so that it was impossible to put a ferry-boat on it. Many people wanted to cross it and the old monk told Opherus that he could serve Jesus by using his magnificent strength to carry people across the river. He did that and he was very happy doing it. Then one wild night a little child came asking to be carried across the river. Opherus did not want to go out on a night like that, but he was kind and he told the child to get on to his back. He began the crossing and somehow the child got heavier and heavier until Opherus could hardly stumble through the storm. At last he got to the other side. He dropped his passenger from his back and behold! it was not a child but a man. "Who are you, sire?" asked Opherus. And the stranger answered, "I am Christ. I wanted to cross the river and because you carried Me you will no longer be called Opherus, but *Christopherus*, not the burden-carrier, but the *Christ-carrier* because you helped Me." Christopher had thought that he was only helping and serving some little child, but really he was helping and serving Jesus. That is exactly what Jesus said. He said, "As you did it to one of the least of these my brethren, you did it to me" (Matthew 25:40).

Jesus said that He Himself came not be be served, but to serve (Matthew 20:28). He came into the world to help, to heal, to comfort and to save others. He still wants people helped; and now He has to find people to carry on the work He began. So every time we serve others we are fellow-workers of God.

God's Fellow-workers

There is no greater honour than to have a share, however small, in some great work. There is no greater privilege than to be the assistant to some great man. It is our great honour that it is possible for us to be the fellow-workers of God. He needs us so that through us He can carry out His purposes. He needs us to tell others about Jesus. He needs us to show others what the Christian life is and what it means to be a Christian. He needs us to help those who have need of help. If we do these things we, too, will be the fellow-workers of God.

QUESTIONS FOR DISCUSSION

1. Are there any in our parish who might be persuaded to come with us to Church? How may we persuade them?

2. If our duty is to show others what the Christian life is like, what kind of life should we be living?

3. In what ways can we help others, as Jesus would wish them to be helped?

Chapter 11

BE THE SALT OF THE EARTH

When Jesus was speaking to His men about the kind of life they ought to live and the kind of people they ought to be, He said to them, "You are the salt of the earth" (Matthew 5:13). That is a phrase which has become part and parcel of our everyday language. When we wish to describe a man who lives a fine and a useful life, we often say of him, "He is one of those people who are the salt of the earth." We mean that life would be infinitely poorer without people like that. Let us see if we can find out what Jesus meant us to be when He said that we, too, must be the salt of the earth.

The Demand for Purity

In the ancient world, in the time of Jesus, people always connected salt with *purity*. They said that salt came from the two purest things of all—the sun and the sea. Salt was the first of all the sacrifices to the gods, and the Jews always salted their sacrifices before they offered them to God. To them salt was the only thing which was always pure enough to be an offering to God. So then, if we are to be the salt of the earth we must first of all be pure.

There are three great departments of our life and in them all we must be pure. (1) We must be pure in our *actions*. There was a great Danish sculptor called Thorwaldsen. He had carved a very famous statue of Jesus. He was offered a commission by the French government to carve a statue of the Roman goddess Venus. They offered him a great deal of money to do so. His answer was, "The hands which carved the figure of Christ can never carve the figure of a heathen goddess." He would not soil his hands by touching any lesser thing. The Psalmist said that if we are going to approach God we must have *clean hands* (Psalm 24:4). There is one way in which we can keep all our actions pure. A famous preacher, giving advice to other preachers, said that once a preacher has written a sermon the best thing he can do with it is to take it in his hands and kneel down in a corner of his room and offer it to God. If we try to do everything in such a way that we could take it and offer it to God then we will keep all our work fine and all our actions pure.

(2) We must be pure in our *words*. Nearly everywhere we go we hear people speaking words that are not pure. Sometimes they use oaths; sometimes they repeat stories which are not clean. It is very easy for us to catch the taint and the infection. One of the oddest experiences in the world is to hear a recording of your own voice. It is true to say that hardly anyone recognises his own voice. In a certain theological college, the Department of Practical Training uses a tape-recording machine, and every student has to preach a sermon into it and then it is played back to him. In that way the students can see the faults in their speech and the irritating mannerisms they may have and so they are helped to cure them. One of the best ways to keep our words clean is to remember that God hears them. No matter where we are in this world or in any other world we can never get away from God. The Psalmist said, "Even before a word is on my tongue, lo, O Lord, thou knowest it altogether" (Psalm 139:4). It will help to keep our words pure if we remember that God always hears.

(3) We must be pure in our *thoughts*. This is the hardest of all, for thoughts are very difficult to control. We can easily test this. Sit down and try to think of one thing and *one thing only* for just two minutes. There is hardly anybody who can do it. If we try it, we find that this, that and the next thing come flashing into our minds; that this, that and the next picture rise before our eyes; that, however hard we try, it is almost impossible to keep our thoughts on one thing and one thing only for even as short a time as two minutes. There is only one way to avoid evil thoughts. It is not to say, "I will not think of this or that." If we do that it only fixes our thoughts more firmly upon it. It is to think good thoughts so

that the good ones drive out the evil ones. If we fix our thoughts on fine things, the lower things will not trouble us any more. So, then, first of all, if we are to be the salt of the earth we must be pure in action and in word and in thought.

The Demand for Usefulness

The second thing that people always remembered about salt in the time of Jesus was its *usefulness*. There was a Latin proverb which said *"Nihil utilius sale et sole,"* there is nothing more useful than salt or sun. In fact the Greeks used to call salt *divine*, because they believed rightly that it was so essential that life could not go on without it. So, then, if we are to be the salt of the earth we must be *useful*.

There are two places where it is possible for us to be useful. (1) We can be useful *at home*. Some people look on their homes as places that they use. They expect to come in and go out and find everything ready and everything done for them. They are just passengers who do not help things on at all. There was a very famous author who was brought up in a very poor home. In that home it was always a struggle to get enough food to eat. When he was quite small he got his first job as a message boy and he took his first pay, just a few shillings, home and gave it to his mother. That night he sat down to tea. On the table there was a new loaf of bread. His mother pointed at the loaf and said to him, "You see that loaf? Well, *your* money bought it for us." That author tells us that he never felt so proud in his life. He felt for the first time that he had been of use, that he had put something into the house and home instead of always taking things out. There are many ways we can be useful at home. We must see to it that we are not just selfish passengers who never try to be of use.

(2) We can be useful in the *Church*. The Church tends to have two kinds of members. There is the member who looks on the Church as existing only to provide him with help. But there is also the member who sees the Church as something that needs his service. The first member thinks in terms of what the Church can do for him; the second member

thinks in terms of what he can do for the Church. If there is a job to be done he is always on the spot. It is obvious that if all the Church members were like the first one, the Church would be in a bad way; but if all its members were like the second one, the Church would be much nearer what God means it to be. So, then, if we are to be the salt of the earth, we must be of use.

The World's Preservative

The third thing that impressed the ancient world about salt was *its power to preserve things against corruption*. Salt is the oldest preservative in the world; it was the first thing to be used to keep meat and fish from going bad. The Greeks used to say that salt was able to put a new soul into a dead thing. So, then, salt preserves against corruption. If we are to be the salt of the earth we must be like a preservative.

Long ago the greatest empire in the world was the Roman Empire. The strange thing was that for almost three hundred years the Roman Empire persecuted the Christians and killed them and threw them into prison. Then there came the time round about A.D. 330. Anyone could see that there was something very seriously wrong with the Empire. It was obviously breaking up. Away on the frontiers the barbarians were pressing in. Within the Empire there was graft and dishonesty everywhere. Marriage was despised; the home and the family were being destroyed; the Empire seemed rotten at the heart. Then there came to power an Emperor called Constantine. He saw that for Rome there was only one hope and that one hope was Christianity. So he decided that the Empire must stop persecuting the Christians and that Christianity must become the religion of the whole Roman Empire, which at that time was practically the whole world. So he wrote a letter to the leaders of the Christian Church and in it he said, "I am handing over to you the body of the world labouring under grievous sickness that you may cure it." He saw in Christianity and in the Christian Church the one power which could be an antiseptic against the poison of immorality and dishonesty and corruption in the world. That

was the Church being called upon to be the salt of the
earth.

We must be like that. We all know that there are some
people in whose company it is easy to be bad and others in
whose company it is easy to be good. There are some people
who encourage us to do and say the questionable things;
and there are others in whose presence no one would dream
of saying or doing a mean thing. In any company, wherever
we may happen to be, we have to be the kind of people in
whose presence impure things are not said and improper
things are not done. If we are in a company where that kind
of thing happens we may not be able to say anything about
it, but we can at least get up and walk away. This is another
of these things in which there are a great many people who
are only waiting for a lead. Most people do not want to
listen to dirty things or to do questionable things. But they
listen to them and do them because they are afraid to be thought
different, but, if someone gives them a lead, they follow to
the better things. If we are going to be the salt of the earth
we must be the kind of people in whose presence the unclean
things cannot live.

Giving Flavour to Life

The last thing about salt is something which everyone knows
—*salt gives flavour to things*. Things cooked without salt are
dull and insipid and tasteless and even sickening. A pinch
of salt gives flavour to things. Christianity is the thing which
gives flavour to life. There are still people who seem to think
that Christianity takes the flavour out of life, that it consists in
doing all the things you do not want to do and not doing all
the things you do want to do, that happiness and Christianity
do not go together at all. It is just the other way round.
When Sir Wilfred Grenfell was out in Labrador he wanted a
volunteer to go out as a nursing sister to his hospital. One
girl volunteered. He wrote to her and said, "We can't offer
you much money, but if you come out here and help the sick
and nurse the lonely you will have the time of your life." It
is quite clear that our Christianity should make us happier

and stronger than ever we were before; and above all it gives us the thrill of working for Jesus and of living with Him. A Christian should literally be the life and soul of any society in which he finds himself. If we are going to be the salt of the earth we must be happy ourselves and bring happiness to others.

The Salt of the Earth

Jesus said that His followers must be the salt of the earth. Salt is the purest of all things and His followers must be pure in action, in word and in thought. Salt is the most useful and essential of all things. We must aim to be useful and not useless in the world, to be helpers and not passengers. Salt is the earliest of all preservatives against corruption. We must be such that in our presence no unclean thing can exist. Salt lends flavour to all things. We must be such that we make life happier for ourselves and for others. It is a great ambition to be the salt of the earth and we can only be that when Jesus helps us to fulfil His own command.

Questions for Discussion

1. In what ways can we fall into impure actions, words and thoughts? How can we guard against them?

2. In what ways can we be useful at home and in our Church?

3. What chances do we get to act as an antiseptic and a preservative in the world? How can we combat uncleanness and impurity?

4. How can we help to add flavour to life for others? How can we bring happiness into the lives of others and how can we show them how happy a thing Christianity can be?

Chapter 12

BE A WITNESS TO JESUS CHRIST

As we saw in Chapter 1, after the Resurrection but before the Ascension, Jesus gave his disciples their commission and their task. He said to them, "You shall be my witnesses in Jerusalem and in all Judea and Samaria and to the end of the earth" (Acts 1:8). When the disciples met to choose a man to replace Judas the traitor in the apostolic band, the reason why they chose him was that he was to be a witness to all the things that Jesus said and did and especially to the Resurrection (Acts 1:22). When Jesus met Paul on the Damascus road, He gave to him a new life and a new task, and the new task was to be a witness to all men of the things that he had seen and heard (Acts 22:15). When Peter was describing himself to the friends to whom he wrote his letter, he described himself as an elder and a witness of the sufferings of Christ (1 Peter 5:1). It is the duty of a Christian to be a witness to Jesus. Let us try to see further what that means for us.

A Man who Knows

First and foremost, *a witness is a man who knows the facts at first hand.* If ever you have to be a witness in a law court, the judge will never allow you to repeat what someone else told you; he will compel you to stick to what you know and have seen and have heard yourself. To be a witness is to be a man who has first-hand knowledge. It is to be able to say of something, "This is true and I know it".

For us that means two things. (1) It means that we must know the facts about Jesus. It means that we must know what Jesus said and what Jesus did and what Jesus taught. We must know the facts of Christianity. Suppose a lad is going to be an electrician or a plumber or a baker or a banker or a lawyer or an accountant, he must know the required text-books which tell him about these trades and professions. Now the Bible is the text-book of the Christian. It is what we might call the manual of Christianity. At our work we may often get into arguments with those who are hostile to Christianity and we cannot meet their arguments unless we know the facts about Jesus. Before we can witness to Jesus we must know the story and we must know what Jesus did and taught. It is not enough only to come to Church; we must read the Bible—especially the Gospels and the Book of Acts—for ourselves. Then we will be able to say that we know, not because someone else told us, but because we found it out for ourselves.

(2) But it is not enough to *know about* Jesus; we must also know Jesus. There is a great difference between knowing about a person and knowing a person. We all know about Queen Elizabeth but very few of us know her. Now a real Christian not only knows about Jesus; he also knows Him personally. If anybody had tried to argue with Paul that there never had been any such person as Jesus, Paul would have answered, "But I know that there is such a person; I met Him on the Damascus road." We get to know Jesus by praying to Him and by thinking about Him. This takes time. We will never get to know a person if we are too busy to spend some time meeting him and talking to him. It is just the same with Jesus. If we are to know Him we must make some time each day, when we speak to him and when we think about Him.

There was a man who found it very difficult to pray. He could not find words. He was ill in bed and a friend came to see him and he told his friend about his difficulty. His friend said, "What you want to do is this—just leave this chair that I am sitting on beside your bed, and when you say your prayers turn to the chair and just say to yourself that Jesus is sitting beside you as I am sitting here, and just talk to Him as you are talking to me." The man did not live very long after that. One day they came in and they found him dead—and the chair was drawn up beside his bed and he was lying facing it. If we take the time to do so, we can, by praying to Him and thinking of Him, get to the stage when we not only know about Jesus but when we know Him as our friend.

A Man who is prepared to say that he Knows

But a witness is not only a man who knows, he is also *a man who is prepared to say that he knows*. Sometimes a man knows what the truth is, but he is afraid to tell it. In his heart of hearts he believes in Jesus, but he is afraid to say so. There is an animal called the chameleon. The odd thing about the chameleon is that he is able to change his colour to match his background. Put him on the grass and he turns green; put him on a tree trunk and he turns brown; put him on the sand and he turns the colour of the sand. The idea is that no one will be able to see him because he fades into the background. There are people like that. They take their colour from their company. And if they happen to be in company which does not think and act as they think and act, they conceal what they really believe.

At the battle of Culloden in 1746, the Highland clans were cut to pieces. The cause of the Stuarts was once and for all broken and defeated. After the battle, the Duke of Cumberland, the commander of the government forces, was going about the battlefield. He came on a Highlander sorely wounded. He bent over him and said to him, "To what side do you belong?" With his last strength the Highlander lifted up his broken sword and whispered, "I belong to the king". And at once Cumberland stabbed him to death. He knew that he was asking for death, but he was prepared to witness to his loyalty anywhere. It is our duty not only to know about Jesus and to know Him, but to let others see that we are on His side.

A Man who is prepared to suffer for saying that he Knows

That really means this—that a witness is *a man who is prepared to suffer for saying that he knows*. There is one very interesting thing about the word witness. The Greek word for *witness* is *martus*, and *martus* is also the Greek word for *martyr.* There was a time when to be a witness for Christ and to be a martyr were one and the same thing.

A real witness is always a man who is prepared to stand by the thing he believes to be true even if he has to suffer for it. In the early days of the Church in one sense it would have been the easiest thing in the world for Christians to have escaped imprisonment and death. All they needed to say was that they did not believe in Jesus. Pliny was the governor of the Roman province of Bithynia. There were many Christians there and he was intent on wiping them out. He wrote home to the Emperor and told him of the methods that he followed. When he arrested a Christian he gave him a choice—either worship the Emperor and curse Christ or die. And then he writes: "Real Christians can never be forced to do so". All that the Christian had to do was to speak one word saying that he did not believe in Christ and then he might go free and escape death, but he would not speak it.

When there was persecution in Egypt in the middle of the third century there was a young lad on trial for his faith. It was clear that he was wavering. When they saw him five Roman soldiers ran forward. "Stand fast," they said, "we, too, are Christians." And they died with him. All they needed to do was to keep quiet and they were perfectly safe, but they did not do so. A witness is a man who makes clear what side he is on, even when that means trouble for himself.

Witnessing for Christ

In our day and generation we will not likely have to suffer physical torture or to die for our Christianity, but the duty of being a witness is still laid upon us. There are three spheres of life where we get a special chance to witness for our Christian faith and principles. (1) We get the chance to witness for our Christian principles *at our work*. At his work the Christian is a man who will never offer to anyone anything that is less than his best. It does not matter whether people see it or not, it does not matter whether he is thanked and praised and rewarded or not, he will offer nothing less than his best. Once they were cleaning a vast cathedral and they were working at a part of the stonework which had never been cleaned or touched for hundreds of years. Up there in a dark corner where no one would see it they found on the stone carving of exquisite beauty. Hundreds of years ago some mason had carved it. He knew that no one would ever see it and yet there, even in that dark, unseen corner he did his best. We are living in an age where the whole tendency is to push things through any way, to do as little as we can get away with, to do as little as possible and to get as much as possible, to start late and to finish early. No Christian does that. Other people may do it. He may seem queer and different, but the Christian workman is not thinking of what men think of him; he is thinking of what God thinks of him and he bears his Christian witness by being a workman who always does his best.

(2) We get a chance to witness for our Christian principles at our *sport*. We must never think that being a Christian is confined to Church and to Sunday. It is our duty to take our Christianity on to the playing fields with us. There is the kind of player who is out to win at all costs. If he cannot do it by fair means he will do it by foul. He takes a pride in getting away with some dirty action when the referee or the umpire is not watching. He will not hesitate to foul a man if he thinks he can safely do so. No Christian would do that. We can show our Christianity by being examples of honour in every game that we play. It would be far better never to win a game than to win them all by methods which are not clean.

(3) We get a chance to witness to our Christian principles in our *pleasure*. There are two rules to remember about pleasure. First, it is wrong to find pleasure in anything that will hurt us in body or in mind in the days to come. Second, it is wrong to find pleasure in anything that might hurt or even ruin someone else. Take two cases. A young man should steer clear of drink. He may be able to take it in moderation and it may do him no harm, but what is harmless to him may be ruin to someone else. A young man should steer clear of every form of betting and gambling, even of the pools which

are so common, because he cannot win unless someone else loses. His gain can only come from someone else's loss; and that is not a Christian way of making money. One of the greatest ways in which we can show what side we are on is in what we allow ourselves to do and what we refuse to do in our pleasure.

Witnesses for Christ

Jesus told His men that they must be witnesses for Him. A witness is a man who knows at first hand that a thing is true. We must study our Bibles and especially the Gospels which tell the story of Jesus, so that we may know what Jesus was like and what He said and did. We must find time to pray to Jesus and to think about Him so that we may get beyond knowing about Him and come to know Him as our personal friend. A witness is a man who is not afraid to say what he believes. A witness is a man who will say what he believes even if the saying of it gets him into trouble. At our work we can witness to Christ by being conscientious all the time. At our sport we can witness to Christ by refusing ever to do a mean thing or take a mean advantage. At our pleasure we can witness for Christ by never finding delight in anything that would hurt ourselves or any other person. And if we witness for Christ like that we will one day enter into our reward for Jesus is always true to those who are true to Him.

QUESTIONS FOR DISCUSSION

1. How can we get to know Jesus better?

2. What opportunities do we get to tell people what we believe?

3. What kind of things are we liable to suffer if we are loyal to our Christian principles?

4. In what way must the Christian workman differ from the workman who is not a Christian? In what way must the player who is a Christian be different from the player who is not a Christian? Can you think of any pleasures in which a Christian cannot rightly indulge?

PART 3: GOD'S MEN

Chapter 13

JOHN MARK—THE MAN WHO REDEEMED HIMSELF

In the early days of the Church they had no church buildings such as we have. For one thing, the Christians were far too poor to erect churches. For another, it was against the law to be a Christian, and the Roman government would never have allowed them to build churches, even if they had been able to do so. The result was that the little groups of Christians used to meet in private houses; and if any Christian had a house with a big room in it he would lend that room on the Sunday for the Christian Church service. There was a lady in Jerusalem called Mary; and it was in her house that the Christians used to meet. When Peter was released from prison it was to that house, to the meeting place of the Church, that he first turned (Acts 12:12). Mary had a son called John Mark. John was his Jewish name, the name by which the family and his closest friends would call him; Marcus was his Roman name, the name by which he would be known out in the world, because in those days when the Romans were masters of Palestine, all Jews had two names, one Roman and one Jewish. From his very earliest days Mark came into contact with the great figures of the Church.

Mark gets his Chance

As the years moved on Mark grew up until he was no longer a boy but a young man; and then he got one of the most thrilling chances that has ever come to anyone. The Church decided that the story of Jesus was not something which was to be kept for Jews alone, and they chose two men to begin the tremendous task of taking the gospel out into all the world. These two men were Paul and Barnabas (Acts 13:1-4). Now Barnabas was Mark's uncle and he thought it would be a

grand thing if Mark was to come with them. He was not to
come as a preacher—he was too young for that—he was to
come as a servant (Acts 13:5). The word which is used in
the Greek is a very interesting word. (The Authorised Version
has the word *minister;* nowadays that is misleading. *Minister*
has now a specialised meaning, but in the seventeenth century
when the Authorised Version was made, it meant, perfectly
generally, a *servant*.) The word in the Greek is *huperetes*
(pronounced hoop-ae-ret-aes) and it originally meant a
rower in a trireme; it was the word for the man who pulled
at the great sweeps which drove the triremes through the sea.
So Mark was to be a servant; he was to be like the oarsman
who helped the ship upon its voyage across the sea.

Mark misses his Great Chance

For a while everything went well. When they were in
Cyprus (Acts 13:4-12) everything was easy-going and Mark
was quite content. But after they had made a preaching tour
of Cyprus they came back to the mainland at Perga in
Pamphylia. But, for some reason, Paul did not want to
preach there although it was a populous district. He wanted
to go inland. Now the road inland was a notorious road.
There was quite a narrow coastal strip and beyond that there
was a high plateau. And the road from the coast up to the
plateau was one of the most difficult roads in the world; and
it was also one of the most dangerous because it was haunted
by robbers and brigands. When Paul and Barnabas proposed
to set out on that uphill and perilous road, Mark quit. He
turned and went back home to Jerusalem (Acts 13:13). An
old Greek called Chrysostom, commenting on this passage,
said that Mark wanted his mother! Anyhow Mark had not
the courage to face a road like that and he became a quitter.

A Quarrel about Mark

Paul and Barnabas went ahead by themselves. No one
could ever imagine Paul turning back. They made a long
missionary journey (Acts 13 and 14). Then they came back

to Jerusalem and told the Christians there all about it (Acts
15:1-4). But Paul could never be at rest while there were men
who had not heard about Jesus and he and Barnabas decided
to start out again. And now there comes a very sad incident.
Barnabas wanted to take Mark with them again; after all,
he was Mark's uncle; but Paul refused. He would have
nothing to do with the young man who had quit. The
difference was so sharp that Paul and Barnabas parted
company and never, so far as we know, worked together again
(Acts 15:36-41). So at this stage Paul had nothing but
contempt for Mark and regarded him as hopeless when it
came to doing some real work for Jesus.

The Great Change

For the next fifteen years Mark vanishes from the scene
completely. We know all about what Paul was doing; but
the New Testament tells us not one word about Mark.
Legend and tradition say that he went to Alexandria and
founded the Christian Church in Egypt; but we know nothing
definite. And then quite suddenly Mark reappears again.
By this time Paul has been arrested and imprisoned; he has
been brought to Rome and is awaiting trial and almost certain
death. In prison he kept on writing letters to his beloved
Churches; and he wrote a letter to the Church at Colosse.
In it there comes a most surprising sentence. "Aristarchus
my fellow-prisoner greets you, and Mark the cousin[1] of Barnabas (concerning whom you have received instructions—if he
comes to you, receive him)" (Colossians 4:10). Something
has happened. The lad whom Paul once called a quitter is
sharing his imprisonment; and Paul is going to send him as a
trusted messenger to Colosse.

At the same time as Paul wrote to the people of Colosse he
sent a private note to his friend Philemon and in it there is
another surprising sentence. Paul sends Philemon good
wishes from Mark, Aristarchus, Demas and Luke, whom he
calls "my *fellow-workers*". Mark the quitter is now a fellow-

[1] This relationship is wide. Most people believe that Barnabas and Mark
were uncle and nephew.

worker. More than that, he had begun by being a servant, like the man who pulled at the oar; now Paul speaks of him as a full partner in his work. But we can go further even than that. Paul was in prison in Rome for at least two years (Acts 28:30, 31); and during these years we have seen that he used Mark as his messenger. Very near the end, perhaps within days of his death, he wrote to Timothy, his right-hand man; and near the end of the letter he says: "Do your best to come to me soon. Luke alone is with me. Get Mark and bring him with you; for he is very useful in serving me" (2 Timothy 4:9-11). The one person Paul wanted at the end was Mark. No one will ever know how he did it, but Mark was the man who redeemed himself.

Mark and Peter

But the New Testament gives us one more glimpse of Mark and from other sources we know just a little more about him. When Peter was writing to his friends from Rome he sent good wishes from Mark, who was so near and so dear to him that he called him *my son* (1 Peter 5:13). (Babylon stands for Rome; cp. Revelation 17:5. Rome was so cruel to the Christians that they nicknamed her Babylon, because it was Babylon which had cruelly carried the Jews away into exile.) Now we know that Mark did something quite outstanding for Peter. There was an old scholar named Papias who lived about 100 years after and he tells us this. "Mark, who was Peter's interpreter, wrote down accurately, though not in order, all that he recollected of what Christ had said or done. For he himself was not a hearer of the Lord nor an original follower of His; he followed Peter, as I have said, at a later date, and Peter adapted his instruction to practical needs, without any attempt to give the Lord's words systematically. So that Mark was not wrong in writing down some things in this way from memory, for his one concern was neither to omit or to falsify anything that he had heard." This indeed was Mark's great work. Peter was a fisherman, not used to writing; he was too busy preaching to write very much or very often; but Mark wrote down the things that Peter used

to tell about Jesus; and what Mark wrote is the Gospel we
read and which bears his name to this day. The man who
was once dismissed as a quitter was the man Paul wanted
at the end and the man who preserved for us and for all the
world the things that Peter used to preach.

The Lad who had a Good Home

Let us now gather up what we know about Mark. First,
we know this: *Mark was a lad who came from a good home.*
He had a good start in life; he had a fine mother in whose
house the Christians met. We can never be thankful enough
for a good home. In the early Church there was a very famous
man called Augustine. But when he was a young man he
was anything but good. His mother, Monica, was very
worried about him and she used to pray for him and weep
for him. She was so worried that she went to a wise old
bishop and told him her worries and her prayers. He said to
her: "It is impossible that a child of such prayers and tears
should perish". His mother's prayers saved him. Thomas
Carlyle, the great writer, who was born in Ecclefechan, in
Scotland, used to say that what kept him right was his mother's
voice still coming to him from the kirk-yard in Ecclefechan
and still saying to him across the years, "Trust in God and
do the right".

In World War I a young soldier was talking to his padre.
He was telling the padre how he was often nervous and worried
and afraid; but in the strangest way he always felt calm and
happy and peaceful about ten o'clock at night. He asked the
padre if he could explain this. The padre said: "I wouldn't
be surprised if that was the time when your mother was
saying her prayers and that just then she was praying for you".
The lad wrote home and found that indeed this was so. If we
have a good home and good parents there is no greater gift
from God; and we should never forget to thank Him for them.

The Lad who was too Dependent

But it may well be that *Mark was the lad who got too
dependent on the people who were so kind to him at home.*

When it came to a difficult job he could not face it and he ran away home. Although we can have no greater gift than a good home, it is also our duty to grow up strong and independent and able to stand on our own feet. That is what our parents want. When the Black Prince was fighting at the battle of Crécy a messenger came to his father, King Edward, to say that the Prince was hard pressed. "Is he unhorsed or wounded?" demanded the king. "No," said the messenger, "but he is up against it." "Then," said the king, "let him fight on himself and let him win his spurs." It should be our aim that in the end we do not go on taking things out of our homes, but that we start taking them into our homes; that we should not always depend on the people at home doing things for us, but that we should do things for them; that we should make ourselves so independent that we can help them as much as they have helped us. As we have already said we cannot thank God too often or too much for a good home, but a good home should not make us soft and flabby as at first it made Mark. It should make us strong and able to do things for ourselves and for others.

The Lad who redeemed Himself

But above all, *Mark was the lad who redeemed himself.* Mark had his failure, but he set out to redeem that failure. Mark made his mistake, but he set out to correct that mistake. It must have hurt Mark to the quick when Paul contemptuously refused to have him with him on the second journey, but Mark there and then set out to prove to Paul that he was a better man than Paul thought. We must never let a failure get us down. When the publishing firm who published his books failed, and when he lost every penny he had, Sir Walter Scott said, "No man is going to say 'Poor fellow' to me. My own right hand will pay the debt." And he set to and paid it. When Disraeli, who was one of our greatest Prime Ministers, made his first speech to Parliament, the House laughed him down. As he sat down he said, "You may laugh me down today but the day will come when I will make you listen to me". It did; the day came when they made the man whom they had laughed down Prime Minister. We must never let a failure discourage us or knock the heart out of us. We must use a failure as a spur to do better. Mark was the man who redeemed himself; and anyone can do the same, with the help of Jesus.

QUESTIONS FOR DISCUSSION

1. Why do you think Mark turned and went home when Paul and Barnabas decided to go up from the sea coast on to the plateau?

2. In the argument about taking Mark with them on the second journey, do you think Paul or Barnabas was right?

3. What do we owe to our homes? What can we do for our homes? How can we show our gratitude for all that we have received?

Chapter 14

BARNABAS—THE MAN WHO WAS KIND

There is no kindlier soul in all the New Testament than Barnabas. Men read his character in his very name—"Barnabas," writes Luke, "which means, Son of encouragement" (Acts 4:36). It is characteristic of the Hebrew language that it is deficient in adjectives. Because of that it often uses "Son of ——" plus an abstract noun instead of an adjective. So in Luke 10:5, 6, Jesus sends out the seventy disciples and tells them to send their peace upon a house if "a son of peace is there". By the phrase "a son of peace" Jesus meant a kindly, peaceable man. So when Barnabas is called a "son of encouragement" it means that he was a sympathetic, consoling, kindly, encouraging person. Barnabas on every occasion in which he appears in the New Testament is being kind to someone.

The Man who delighted to serve Others

We meet him first in Acts 4:34-37. The early Church was a society in which people knew the joy of sharing things. No man who had enough could bear to see someone else having too little and so they pooled all they had and shared it with each other. Barnabas, we are told, was a Levite. That in itself is suggestive. The Levites' work was in the Temple, but it was work which was seldom seen. It was the priests who occupied the limelight. It was the priests who carried out the great sacrifices which everyone could see and admire. The duty of the Levites was to sweep the floors, to open and shut the doors, to act as temple police, to do all the menial jobs in the holy place. But they were proud to do it because they were doing it for God.

In the Roman Empire the greatest honour that a city could have was to house the temple where Caesar was worshipped as a god. The title that such cities received was the Greek word *Neokoros*, which means *temple-sweeper*. They felt it an honour to be the temple-sweeper of the sacred shrine of Caesar. That is what the Levites felt about their work for God, and Barnabas was a Levite. He was from the beginning a man whose one delight was to serve. Now Barnabas was a wealthy man and he had an estate. But he looked around upon his fellow members of the Christian Church and saw many of them who were slaves, many of them who were poor, many of them who were often hungry. Thereupon the kindly Barnabas made a decision. He sold his land and took the money and laid it at the disciples' feet and told them to use it to help others who never had enough.

We must all think what we are going to do with our possessions. Are we going to keep them all to ourselves? Are we going to be in life to see how much we can get out of it? Are we going to live on the principle that it does not matter what happens to others so long as we are comfortable and at ease? To be honest, that is what most people do. Or are we going to say, Whatever I have, God gave it to me not to keep, but to share? Are we going to think more of what others have not than of what we have? That is what Barnabas did, and that is what Jesus did. Though He was rich, yet for our sakes He became poor. If we are to be like Barnabas and if we are to be like Jesus, to give and not to get will be our motto.

The Man who thought the Best

The next time we meet Barnabas he was doing a very brave thing (Acts 9:26, 27). There was a time when Paul had been the greatest persecutor of the Church; then he had met Christ upon the Damascus road, and he became the devoted servant of the Master whom he had once persecuted. For a while he stayed in Damascus preaching there, and then his enemies tried to kill him and he had to flee for his life. He went to Jerusalem, and there the Church received him with the gravest suspicions. We cannot altogether blame them. It was hard to believe that the man who had once been the Church's bitterest enemy now wanted to be the Church's servant. We do not know what might have happened to Paul had it not been for Barnabas. But in this unhappy situation Barnabas came forward and took Paul by the hand and stood sponsor for him. Barnabas trusted the man of whom everyone else was suspicious. He stood up to defend the man whom everyone else wished to condemn.

The difference was this—the other Christians thought the worst about Paul, but Barnabas believed the best. It is a great gift to think the best of others, but usually it is human nature to think the worst. Collie Knox tells of a thing that happened to him in World War I. He was an airman and was badly smashed up in a flying accident. He was dining with a friend one day in London and they were both in civilian clothes. A girl came up and handed each of them a white feather. A white feather was a sign of cowardice and people used to give them to people who, as they thought, ought to be in the army. But what that girl did not know was that Collie Knox had been smashed up flying with the Royal Flying Corps and that his friend that very morning had been decorated for gallantry by the King. The girl with the feather thought the worst and she was very, very mistaken.

Jesus had the most wonderful power of thinking the best of other people. Matthew was a tax-gatherer, a traitor to his country who had sold himself into the service of the Romans, but Jesus saw in him an apostle and a man whom He could use. Peter was an unstable and an erratic character, but Jesus saw in him one on whom He could found His Church. It is very easy to think the worst about other people. Jesus always thought the best. So did Barnabas. So must we.

The Man who opened Wide the Door

The next time we meet Barnabas he is just the same (Acts 11:19-26). Some of the Christians had found their way down to Antioch. Antioch was at that time the third greatest city in the world. Up to this time the Christians had all been Jews. Now the Jews believed that they were the chosen people, and that God had no use for any other people; and

it had not yet struck the Christians that Christianity was
something for everybody and that Jesus was the gift of God
to every man. But some of the Christians who had gone to
Antioch started to preach the gospel not only to Jews, but to
Gentiles, too. News of this came back to Jerusalem and they
did a very wise thing—they sent Barnabas to Antioch to see
what was happening. When Barnabas got there and saw how
Jews and Gentiles alike were listening to the word of God
and becoming the followers of Jesus he never hesitated for a
moment as to what to do. He said, "Open the doors of the
Church and let them all come in, because we want them all."
Barnabas was the man with the heart that was big enough to
love everyone.

When you come to think about it there are really only two
kinds of people—those who shut doors and those who open
them. There are the people who are quite content with their
own little clique. They do not want strangers. They make
strangers feel out of it and never give them a welcome. They
do not want to share their games, their activities, their
pleasures with anyone else. That is not Christian. The real
Christian welcomes all strangers and opens the door to them.
That is what Barnabas did and that is what we must do.

The Man who took the Second Place

The next time we meet Barnabas he is just starting out on a
very big job. The Church at Antioch had even wider ideas.
It saw not only a city for Christ; it saw a whole world for
Christ; and it decided to send out Paul and Barnabas to bring
the message of Christ to all men, or at least to begin that task
(Acts 13). Now it is clear that at the beginning of that mission
Barnabas was the man in charge. His name comes first—it is
Barnabas and Paul (Acts 13:2). The first place they went to
was Cyprus and it is quite clear that from the very first Paul
took the lead (read verses 4-12). By the time they had
completed their work in Cyprus and were about to leave, it is
no longer a case of Barnabas and Paul; it is Paul and his
company (Acts 13:13). It is Paul who is in the lead and
Barnabas is not even mentioned. And yet we hear no word

of complaint from Barnabas. He was quite content to stand back and let Paul take the first place.

There is nothing more hurting than to be passed over. There is nothing more difficult than to take the second place when once you held the first place, or when you were expecting to get the first place. In America there was a minister called Dr. Spence. At one time his church was packed with people. But bit by bit the congregations, after many years, began to get smaller. A young minister came to the church across the street and he got all the crowds and Dr. Spence's church was almost empty. One night it was very empty. Dr. Spence looked around and said, "I wonder where all the people have gone?" There was a dead silence because no one wanted to tell him, and then someone very apologetically said, "I think, Dr. Spence, that they are all across the street hearing the new minister." "Is that so?" said the old man. "Then I think we had better join them." And he led his people across the road to the other church. There was no jealousy, no bitterness. He was quite prepared to stand back and to take the second place.

There is often trouble in a church because someone is passed over for office or because someone does not get his or her place. Barnabas could step down and never breathe a word of complaint. He could take the first place or the second place equally willingly. It did not matter to him so long as the work was done. It is that kind of person that Jesus needs. We must try to be like that.

The Man who could Forgive

The last time we meet Barnabas in the Book of Acts he is still the same (Acts 15:36-41). When Barnabas and Paul had first set out from Antioch they had Mark with them as their helper. For some reason or other, when they had reached Perga and were aiming to make an expedition inland up into the central plateau, Mark quit and went back home. Now Paul and Barnabas were laying plans for another campaign for Christ. Barnabas wanted to take Mark with them again;

but Paul refused point blank. He said he had no use for quitters; and the result was that Paul and Barnabas split company, and Barnabas took Mark and Paul took Silas and they went their own ways. Barnabas was the man who could forgive.

It is hard to forgive when you have been let down. Mr. Gladstone was one of the greatest of all British Prime Ministers. He did many great things, but one who knew him well tells a thing about him that was greater than the things that far more people knew about. He was to make a speech in Parliament. He was dependent on his private secretary for giving him the correct figures and statistics, but the figures he was given were quite wrong. Gladstone, of course, had his enemies and his enemies took their chance and tore him to pieces, making him look very foolish. His private secretary fully expected to be dismissed on the spot—as, indeed, he deserved to be. But Gladstone never spoke an angry word to him. He simply said that anyone could make a mistake and never held it against him. The private secretary had let him down, but he could forgive.

Nobody ever let Jesus down so badly as Peter did. Just when Jesus needed him most Peter denied Him and failed Him. And yet when Jesus rose from the dead, He sent a special message to Peter (Mark 16:7) and He made one of His first appearances to Peter (Luke 24:34). Jesus did not hold it against him.

In the seventeenth century there was a lad called Tom Ellwood. He made up his mind that he would do a very difficult thing—that he would become a Quaker. His father sent him on business to Oxford and for a while he was able to show his colours courageously and to make it clear where he stood. But as he was going home, all of a sudden he saw some old acquaintances coming down the road. He felt that he could not meet them and risk being laughed at. So he slipped down a side road and out of the town by a round-about way. He was very troubled for having, as he said, "shamed the Cross". "But," he said, "the Lord looked on me with a tender eye and He was graciously pleased to pass it by, and speak peace to me again." Jesus did not hold it against him.

There is nothing harder than to learn to forgive and not to hold it against someone who has hurt or wronged us. But what would happen to us if Jesus held against us all the times we had hurt Him or been disloyal to Him? Jesus forgives. Barnabas could forgive and we must ask Jesus' help to enable us to do the same.

Barnabas

It is only every now and then that the New Testament gives us little glimpses of Barnabas, but even from them we see that he must have been a very lovely character. He was the man who delighted to serve others. He was the man who always thought the best of others. He was the man who could take the second place and bear no ill-will to the man who surpassed him. He was the man who could forgive and never hold anything against the man who let him down. There is no better example than Barnabas, the man who was kind!

QUESTIONS FOR DISCUSSION

1. In what practical ways can we help others?

2. Think of ways in which we think the worst of others. How can we cure ourselves of that habit?

3. Think of ways in which we may have to take the second place when we expected the first, and when we thought we deserved the first. How can we keep ourselves from resentment if that should happen?

4. Think of the things that are difficult to forgive. How can we learn to forgive?

Chapter 15

LUKE—THE GOOD COMPANION

We do not know a great deal about Luke, but what we do know makes us think that he must have been a most interesting and a most lovable person. First of all, let us collect the facts about him.

He was the author of two New Testament books. He wrote The Gospel according to St. Luke and The Acts of the Apostles. It is interesting to remember that all the other New Testament books were written by Jews, and that Luke is therefore the only Gentile among all the New Testament authors.

He was a doctor by profession. When Paul was writing to his friends at Colosse, he sent them greetings from Luke, the beloved physician (Colossians 4:14). Even if we had not known this, we could have guessed it, because Luke has a way of using medical words. To take one example. Three gospel writers tell us of the saying of Jesus that it is easier for a camel to go through the eye of a needle than for a rich man to enter the Kingdom of God (Matthew 19:24; Mark 10:25; Luke 18:25). Now Matthew and Mark both use the Greek word *raphis* and *raphis* is the usual Greek word for a needle, because it means a *tailor's* or a *housewife's needle*. But Luke uses a different word. He uses *belone* and *belone* is a *surgeon's needle*, the kind of needle that a surgeon uses when he is carrying out an operation. When Luke, the doctor, thought about needles, it was the surgeon's needle that came first to his mind and to his lips.

He was one of Paul's travelling companions. Here we find a very interesting thing. If we read the Book of Acts we will find that large parts of it are told in the *third person plural*. We read that "They did this" and "They did that". But every now and again we come upon a passage that is written in the *first person plural*, and which says, "We did this" and "We

did that". Scholars call these the "we passages of Acts".
We find them in Acts 16:10-17; 20:5-16; 21:1-18; 27:1-29.
This means that Luke was actually there on these occasions.
Perhaps he kept a diary and when he came to write Acts he
transcribed these parts from his diary. At any rate, when
we read these "we passages" we can read them with a double
interest because they are what we would now call eye-witness
accounts.

Luke was Paul's companion in his last imprisonment. When
Paul wrote the letter to Philemon he was in prison in Rome
awaiting trial and he sends greetings from Luke who was with
him (Philemon 24). When he wrote 2 Timothy he was waiting for death and his life was almost at an end, and everybody else had left him, but Luke was still there (2 Timothy
4: 11).

These are all the definite facts that we know about Luke,
but these facts tell us a great deal about what kind of man he
was.

A Humble Man

First and foremost, *Luke was a humble man.* He wrote
two whole books of the New Testament and *never mentioned
his own name.* He was quite content to remain unknown. If
he had wished he could have written himself up. No doubt
he could have made himself out to be something of a hero
and a most important person, but in his books there is not a
word about himself. No one really likes a conceited person
who is always talking about himself. Everyone likes a modest,
humble person, and Luke was just that.

The really great men are quite content to be forgotten.
They are far more interested in the job they are doing than in
themselves, and they do not care who gets the credit so long
as the job is done. Once a great man called Oberlin was
journeying across a pass in the Alps in wintertime. He was
caught in a blizzard and lost his way completely. He would
certainly have died unless another traveller had come upon
him and guided and helped him. When they got to safety

Oberlin wished to reward this man, but he would take nothing. "Well," said Oberlin, "if you will take no reward, at least tell me your name and I'll remember you always in my prayers." But the traveller would not even tell Oberlin his name. Oberlin pressed him. The traveller said, "I'll tell you my name on one condition. I'll tell you it if you tell me the name of the Good Samaritan." Oberlin said, "I can't. No one knows his name." "Well," said the traveller, "you don't need to know mine." He did not want thanks or praise or fame; all he wanted to do was to help.

During London's bad blitzes in World War II a building was hit by a bomb and crashed in ruins. When the rescue squad arrived, they found a man pinned at the very foot of a long deep tunnel of masonry, bleeding to death and in great pain. A little doctor was passing. He said, "I'll go down and help the man. I'll give him morphia." Now the ruins were tottering and there was serious danger of fire. Further, the tunnel in the masonry was so narrow that even if the doctor got down to the bottom of it he could not stoop to tend the man. The doctor said, 'Get a crane. Tie me to it by the heels and let me down head first." They let him down head first, and down he went and gave the man morphia to ease his pain. When they hauled him up, he said, "I'll come again about six o'clock in the morning and give him another jag." Back he came. Still they had not been able to get at the man, and once again they let the doctor down head first and once again he helped the man. That was an act of heroism and, the point is, to this day *no one knows that doctor's name because he would not tell anyone*. He did not want a medal or a citation or a paragraph in the newspapers. All he wanted was to help.

We have always to remember it is not we, but the job, that matters. Once Toscanini, the greatest conductor in the world, was rehearsing a Beethoven symphony. After hours of toil he at last achieved with his orchestra a wonderful performance. The first violinist leant over to his neighbour and whispered, "If he scolds us after that I'll jump up and push him into the pit!" But Toscanini was quite quiet for a moment or two and then he said "Who am I? I am nobody. Who are you? You are nobody. *It is Beethoven—he is everything!*" Toscanini did not want himself praised and publicised, he did not want the orchestra to stand out. All that mattered was that people should hear how lovely Beethoven's music can be.

It does not matter whether or not people know our names and thank and praise us, so long as they see Jesus in us. Someone said that so many of the greatest men "forgot themselves into immortality". Like Luke we must be modest and humble, and always keep ourselves out of the centre of the picture.

The Good Companion

Another thing that we can tell about Luke is that he was *a good travelling companion*. As we have seen, he was often with Paul on his journeys and he must have been a good companion or Paul would never have taken him with him. If that is so he must have had certain qualities.

A good traveller must have two great virtues. First, *he must always be willing to think of the other man as much as of himself.* He must learn to match his stride to that of the other man, to lengthen it or shorten it as the case may be. He must be prepared to rest when the other man wants to rest, and to press on when he wants to press on. He must be prepared to agree about the road that they will take, and the places where they will spend the night and the number of miles they will do each day. That man is a hopeless travelling companion who never thinks of anything but of what *he* wants to do and where *he* wants to go. A good companion must learn to consider others, not just as much, but even more than himself.

Boswell used to say that one of the great arts in meeting people is the art of *accommodation*. Paul said that he had become all things to all men so that he could win them for Jesus (1 Corinthians 9:20-22). If we are going to be good companions, we must try to get alongside other people, to think things with their minds, to feel things with their feelings.

Considerateness is one of the most valuable qualities in the world.

Second, a *good travelling companion must be able to take things as they come.* If a man is up and down, easily depressed and discouraged, gets upset by little things, he is no good as a travelling companion. A good companion must be able to take the rough with the smooth, to climb the hills and walk the level, to face the sunshine and the rain, the calm weather and the gale.

Marcus Aurelius was one of the great Stoic Roman Emperors and the Stoics prided themselves on taking everything as it came. When he was dying, one of his guardsmen asked him what the password was for the palace guard that night. He answered, "Equanimity." *Equanimity* means *equal mindedness.* It describes the frame of mind which can take success and disappointment, and happiness and sadness, and carry on.

H. L. Gee quotes an incident from World War II. There had been an air raid on a south of England town. Bombs had been dropped in daylight, and the mother of two children had been agitated because the cinema to which her children had gone had received a direct hit. Rushing to the scene of the disaster, she made enquiries about her little folk, but no one knew anything about them. Finally she hurried home again only to find them sitting by the fire. "Wherever have you been?" she demanded. "Oh," replied the elder child quietly, "Hitler had dropped a bomb on our cinema *so we went to another.*" The child refused to be upset.

The people who are easily rattled, and easily discouraged, the people who are up one day and down the next, the people who, as we say, "can't take it" can never be good companions for the road. Kipling wrote a poem in which he described the real man. He said that one test of a real man was—"If you can meet with Triumph and Disaster, And treat those two impostors just the same". It is a good test.

To be a good companion, Luke must have been always considerate of his fellow-traveller, and he must have been able to take everything as it came. We must be the same.

The Friend to the End

But Luke's loveliest characteristic was that he was *a loyal friend to the very end*. We have seen that Luke was with Paul when Paul was in a Roman prison waiting for death. He was there when everyone else had gone (2 Timothy 4:11). How did Luke get there? That is one of the great stories of the New Testament hidden below the surface.

In Acts 27 we read how Paul was sent a prisoner to Rome, under the care of the centurion Julius, to stand trial for his life. When we read that passage we see that it is a "we passage". So Luke was there. There was only one way in which Luke could get there. It was in the Roman law that a man in Paul's situation might take with him *two personal slaves* as his attendants. In order to accompany Paul on his last journey *Luke must have enrolled himself as Paul's slave*. Loyalty can go no further than that. Luke was so determined to stand by Paul that he was willing to become a slave. Luke was so loyal that when Paul was in prison he would not leave him although he was beyond a doubt risking his own life by sticking to a man who was branded as a criminal. That is the kind of friend everyone would love to have. It is easy enough to get friends who will stand by you when everything is going well. The really valuable friends—and they are rare and hard to find—are the people who will stand by you when everything goes wrong. It is easy to play for a winning team. But the real test comes when the team is losing. Then we see who are the real supporters, and the real team members.

Kipling has a poem which he calls *The Thousandth Man*.

> One man in a thousand, Solomon says,
>   Will stick more close than a brother.
> And it's worth while seeking him half your days
>   If you find him before the other.
> Nine hundred and ninety-nine depend
>   On what the world sees in you,
> But the Thousandth Man will stand your friend
>   With the whole round world agin you.

His wrong's your wrong, and his right's your right,
  In season or out of season.
Stand up and back it in all men's sight—
  With *that* for your only reason!
Nine hundred and ninety-nine can't bide
  The shame or mocking laughter,
But the Thousandth Man will stand by your side
  To the gallows-foot—and after!

This is literally the kind of friend Luke was to Paul, and
that is the kind of friend we must try to be.

Luke

Luke was the Gentile doctor who was the friend of Paul
and the author of two New Testament books. He was a
humble and a modest man, for in his books he never talks
about himself. He was a good travelling companion and he
must have been always considerate and always able to take
things as they came. He was the loyal friend who, for friendship's sake, became Paul's slave and stood by him to the very
end.

QUESTIONS FOR DISCUSSION

1. How can we avoid being conceited?

2. In what ways ought we to learn to be considerate? How
   can we teach ourselves to take things as they come?

3. When are we tempted to let our friends down?

Chapter 16

TIMOTHY—PAUL'S RIGHT-HAND MAN

When we read the letters of Paul there is one name which keeps appearing and re-appearing all the time. It is the name of Timothy. We know very little about the facts of Timothy's life. We know that he came from the district of Lystra and Derbe (Acts 16:1-3) and that is practically all. But we do know that Paul could not have done without him. Again and again he was with Paul when Paul was writing his letters (2 Corinthians 1:1; Philippians 1:1; Colossians 1:1; 1 Thessalonians 1:1; 2 Thessalonians 1:1). Always just at Paul's elbow there was Timothy, ready to help and to stand by. We know that Paul and Timothy were so close together that Paul could speak of him repeatedly as his son (1 Timothy 1:2; 1:18; 2 Timothy 1:2). Most people think that Paul meant Timothy to be his successor in the work of the Church, that Paul, as it were, intended to hand over to Timothy when he died. So then, let us see what we can find out about this young man who was as dear as a son to Paul and whom Paul had destined to shoulder his work when he had to lay it down.

A Good Heritage

First and foremost, Timothy was a lad with a good heritage. Paul speaks of Timothy's faith and then goes on to say that that faith first dwelt in his grandmother Lois and his mother Eunice (2 Timothy 1:5). Timothy had the priceless advantage of a good home. We can never be sufficiently grateful for a good home and for good parents.

Not everyone has that. It is strange to think that Martin Luther's father was so hard and stern to him that he found difficulty in praying the Lord's Prayer, because he did not like to call God "Our Father," because the word *father*

painted to him such a picture of sternness and severity.
Once a Sunday School teacher was telling the story of the
Prodigal Son. She told how the son left home and went away
to the far country; how things went so badly wrong there;
how in the end he made up his mind to come back home.
And when she asked the class, "And what do you think his
father would do when the boy came back home?" Back came
the answer like a shot from one small boy: "Bash him!"
The lad came from a home where he had a father who would
have treated him like that. There are some who never get a
chance at home.

We can never be sufficiently grateful to God for a good home
and kind parents.

A Good Reputation

But not only was Timothy a young man who had a good
heritage, he was also a young man with a good reputation.
He was "well spoken of by the brethren at Lystra and Iconium"
(Acts 16:2). We can be quite sure that Paul would never have
picked him out as his right-hand man if it had not been so.
A good name is the best asset that a young man can have in
all the world. There are two things which get a person a good
name. The first is *honesty*. What everyone is looking for is
someone whom he can trust. The highest compliment that we
can pay anyone is to say "He's absolutely straight". The
second is *obligingness*. Anyone would rather have a quite
ordinary person who does things willingly and with a smile
than a brilliant person who does them with a frown and with
a grudge. People soon get to know the person who, as we
say, will not lift a hand for anyone else, and they have no use
for that kind of person. Timothy had a good name, and a
good name is the most valuable thing in the world.

A Worker

We can see that in another way. In Romans 16:21, when
Paul is sending greetings to his friends, he sends a greeting
from Timothy "my fellow-worker". Timothy was a worker.

People can all be divided into two classes—the shirkers

and the workers. A polar explorer was describing the dogs who had pulled his sledge. He said, "Two of them were pullers and two of them were sooners." "What do you mean?" he was asked. "Well," he said, "two of them were always eager to pull the sledge and two of them would sooner do anything than pull." We all know the kind of person who is always on hand when a job is to be done, and we all know the person who fades away whenever there is a chance of being asked to do anything. And we all know which is the more useful. When Paul was looking for one word in which to describe Timothy he said, "He is my fellow-worker".

The Perfect Messenger

One of the special things about Timothy is that time and time again we read about Paul sending him somewhere. In fact Timothy must have spent most of his life going on expeditions on which Paul sent him. He sent him from Ephesus to Macedonia (Acts 19:22). He sent him from Ephesus to Corinth (1 Corinthians 4:17). He sent him from Athens to Thessalonica (1 Thessalonians 3:2). He planned to send him from Rome to Philippi (Philippians 2:19). Almost every time we read about Timothy he is being sent off somewhere to carry a message from Paul.

Someone has picked out the qualities which make the postage stamp the perfect messenger. First, *the postage stamp sticks to its job*. It is stuck on the envelope and there it stays until it has reached its destination. The person who lets the difficulties beat him never arrives anywhere. A good messenger never gives up until he has delivered his message. During World War II boys were employed as messengers with the Air Raid services. There was a boy called Derek Bellfall who was a messenger in a large English town. He was sent with a message during a blitz when the telephone wires were out of operation and there was no other way to take it. Somehow or other he got through but on the way back he was hit and mortally wounded. When he was found he was just barely able to speak, and when they bent over him he whispered one sentence: "Messenger Bellfall reporting—I have delivered my message". When we are given something to do we should stick at it until it is done.

Second, *the postage stamp goes where it is sent*. Stick it on the envelope and it will go to Edinburgh or London, to Paris or Berlin, to Pekin or Timbuctoo. It will go to the biggest city or the loneliest village. It will go across the street or it will go to the other side of the world. Wherever it is sent it will go. The trouble with most people is that they will work their hardest and their best at the things they like doing, and will do practically nothing to the things they do not like doing. It is that way at school. We are all apt to work at the subjects we like and to neglect the subjects we do not like. It is that way at home. We willingly do the things we like doing, but dodge the things we do not like doing. It did not matter to Timothy where he was sent. He went. It was enough for him that Paul wanted him to go. If we do only the things that we want to do we will not get far in this world. One of the great tests of any person is if he can really put his back into things that he does not want to do. Timothy was a great messenger for Paul because he was ready to go anywhere he was sent and he never gave up until he got there.

A Mind in Tune

There was a reason why Paul so often sent Timothy on his messages and why Timothy was so good a messenger. When Paul was writing to his friends at Philippi and telling them that he was going to send Timothy to them, he said, "I have no one like him, who will be genuinely anxious for your welfare. They all look after their own interests, not those of Jesus Christ" (Philippians 2:20, 21). The great thing about Timothy was that he put the interests of Jesus Christ before his own. In this way Timothy and Paul were of the same mind. That was why he was so good a messenger. He knew just what Paul wanted done, and just how Paul would have wanted him to speak and to act.

It is a great thing for a leader to have someone to send out knowing that that person is one whom he can trust absolutely to do what he would have done himself. Every leader wants people like that. And, above all, Jesus wants people like that. Jesus does not so much want people who will talk about Him as people who will live the kind of life He lived and do the kind of things He did. For instance, He wants people who will help others just as He did. He wants people who will be just as strong and honest and true as He Himself was. He needs messengers today. It is our job to be messengers for Him, and we cannot be that until we take Him into our hearts and become like-minded with Him.

Timothy

Timothy was the lad who came from a good home. Timothy was the lad who had a good name, for we can be sure that he was known to everyone to be honest and obliging. Timothy was the perfect messenger because he always stuck to his job and went wherever he was sent. Timothy was the young man who was like-minded with Paul and whom, therefore, Paul could trust to do his work. Timothy is a good pattern for us to copy.

QUESTIONS FOR DISCUSSION

1. What special dangers are clever people likely to run into? Why is character more important than cleverness?

2. How can we make ourselves willing to work hard even at the things we do not like?

3. What does it mean to be like-minded with Jesus? What are the kinds of things that a person who is like-minded with Jesus will do?

Chapter 17

PHILIP—THE FIRST FOREIGN MISSIONARY

To claim that he was the first foreign missionary is a great claim to make for any man, but that is what Philip was. There are two Philips in the New Testament and we must be careful to distinguish between them. There is the Philip who was one of the twelve whom Jesus chose (Mark 3:18) and there is the Philip who was one of the seven men who were the first office-bearers the Church ever chose (Acts 6). It is this second Philip who was the first foreign missionary.

The Man who was content to accept the Second Place

We first meet Philip in Acts 6 (cf. p. 37). Philip was one of the seven men elected to see to it that the collection of food and money was rightly made and that it was fairly shared out (Acts 6:5). Here, then, we have the first thing that we know about Philip. He was a man who was content to take second place. The people who did the preaching and the teaching would get all the prominence and the publicity; everyone would know them. The people who had to look after the collection and the distribution of the food and the money would have an awkward job that no one would like, and for the doing of which they would get more complaints and criticisms than praise and thanks. But Philip gladly took that job. His one desire was to serve Jesus and he was quite content to serve in any capacity so long as he was serving.

Shakespeare is the greatest dramatist in the world. They tell how Shakespeare left Stratford-on-Avon for London because he was fascinated by the theatre and wanted to write plays. When he got to London the only job he could get was to hold the heads of the horses of the carriages in which the people drove up to the theatre door, but he took it. Later he became an actor. And it was not until after he had accepted these two lesser jobs that he climbed up to the job of writing the plays which he so much wanted to write. Shakespeare, the supreme genius, was prepared to take a lowly job so long as it was getting him near his goal.

That is what Philip was like. He had no pride and no self-conceit. He did not think that any job was too small and too humble so long as he was doing it for Jesus. It might be a boring and unpleasant job; it might be a job that involved him in criticism and trouble; all that mattered to him was that he was doing something for Jesus.

It is never difficult to get people to do things for which they will get prominence and thanks and praise. It is far more difficult to get people for the drab, dull routine jobs which no one will ever notice and which will receive little thanks and no praise. But these jobs must be done. In any machine every littlest screw and nut and cog must be doing its work perfectly or the machine cannot operate. Life is like that and any job done for Jesus' sake is a big job.

The Man who crossed the Barriers

But Philip was too big a man to stay all his life in a small job. And soon his chance came. A very savage persecution of the Christians broke out in Jerusalem, and the Christians had to leave the city. When this happened Philip went down to Samaria and began to preach the gospel there (Acts 8:1-5). This was a tremendous thing. The Jews hated the Samaritans (John 4:9). They despised them and they thought that God had no use for them at all. It was to these despised and hated Samaritans that Philip brought the good news of God and of Jesus. Philip was the man who could cross the barriers, the man who loved people whom others regarded as quite unlovable, the man who wanted to serve the people for whom others had no use.

Rather more than a hundred years ago there lived a lady called Dorothy Dix in East Cambridge in Massachusetts. One Sunday she was asked to help out by taking a Sunday School class in the local prison. She went. She found in one room a group of wretched people shivering in the cold with no fire. She asked why. She was told that these people were lunatics, and that they did not need a fire because they were more like animals than human beings. In those days people who were mentally ill were most cruelly treated. They were shut up in iron cages; they were chained by the neck or by the leg; they were treated worse than wild beasts in a zoo; they were neglected, and even tortured and laughed at by everyone. She determined to help them.

She travelled all over America, journeying more than 60,000 miles and visiting 9,000 of these terrible asylums. She fought all opposition until she got legislation passed which protected and helped these people and gave them decent conditions. She came to Scotland. She met the Lord Provost of Edinburgh and told him that, while many asylums in Scotland were first rate, there was one which was bad. He answered, "Scotland has no need of American invaders to pry into her institutions." She said she would go straight to the Home Secretary with her story. The Lord Provost tried to get there first, but Dorothy Dix went that very night. She saw the Home Secretary, who was so impressed by her story that he told Queen Victoria and action was taken. Dorothy Dix spent her whole life going from country to country, interviewing kings and queens and even the Pope himself. She spent her life helping those for whom no one else had any use.

That is the kind of person Philip was. Everyone else hated the Samaritans. He wanted to help them. It is easy to be friendly with those who are popular and gifted and whom everyone likes. It is a Christian's job to do something for those who are neglected and poor and forgotten by others. Surely there is something that we could do for people whom others forget.

The Man who was Obedient

Philip had good success in Samaria (Acts 8:5-8) but further orders came to him. God sent him a message to go down to the road that led from Jerusalem to Gaza (Acts 8:26). That was a busy road. Gaza was on the great trunk road which led from Egypt to Damascus and there was no telling what people and what caravans a man might meet there. No sooner was Philip told to go than he went. Philip was the man who was obedient.

There is an old legend of the apostle Thomas. Thomas was a carpenter by trade. He was always a gloomy, doubting sort of person. To this day we speak of "Doubting Thomas". After Jesus had died and risen again and gone back to His Father the disciples were deciding where each of them must go and preach the gospel, and Thomas was allocated to India. He said he would not go; he did not understand the language; it was hopeless to ask him to do that job. Now a merchant called Abbanes had come from King Gundaphorus of India to engage a skilled carpenter to come to India. Jesus came down to earth and went to Abbanes and told him that He had a carpenter whom He was willing to sell into his employment. So Jesus wrote out a deed of sale and sold Thomas to Abbanes. Abbanes went to Thomas and confronted him with Jesus and asked, "Is this your master?" "Indeed He is," said Thomas. "Then," said Abbanes, "He has sold you to me." And Thomas' heart was heavy, but he said nothing. But on the next day Thomas rose early and prayed and in his prayer he said to Jesus, "Lord Jesus, I will go wherever you want me to: Thy will be done." When it came to the test Thomas was utterly obedient to Jesus.

Philip was like that. And we must be like that. If we are going to be followers of Jesus, we can no longer do what we like; it must always be what He likes. He will tell us what to do. He will speak to us by the voice of our conscience, and even if we are sent to some hard and difficult task which we do not want to do we have got to do it because Jesus told us to do it. In the Christian life obedience to Jesus comes first of all.

The Man who could explain because He Knew

Away down on the Gaza road Philip met a very interesting man (Acts 8:27-40). He was the Chancellor of the Exchequer of Ethiopia, the modern Abyssinia. He was riding in his chariot and he was reading. In the ancient world, even when people were reading to themselves, they always read aloud; and Philip heard that he was reading Isaiah 53. He asked him if he understood it. The Ethiopian said he could not understand it unless someone explained it. There and then Philip told him how this was a foretelling of Jesus and how Jesus was to die for love of men. He told him the whole story of Jesus, and the Ethiopian there and then became a Christian. Philip was a man who had studied and who had thought things out for himself and who knew what he believed and could explain it to others.

Often at our work we will get into talk about Christianity. Some people will laugh at us; and some people will want to argue with us; and some people will demand why we believe what we do believe. We must be able to tell them. We are not supposed just to sit and listen and accept everything that we are told. We are supposed to think about it and to think it out for ourselves. We must think about things until we can tell people what we believe and why we believe it. If we do that we, too, may have the honour of bringing someone else into the friendship of Jesus.

Philip

Philip was the man who was prepared to take the second place and to do anything so long as he was helping the work of Jesus. He was the man who crossed barriers and who cared for the people for whom no one else cared. He was the man who obeyed God's command without question. He was the man who knew what he believed and who could tell it and explain it to others. He was the first foreign missionary, and if we are like Philip we, too, will have the privilege of helping to bring others to know and to love Jesus.

QUESTIONS FOR DISCUSSION

1. What practical things could we do to help our Church and to help the work of Jesus?

2. In what way could we do something to help people who are neglected? Is there an Old People's Home or a Sana-

torium or a Hospital nearby where we could do something to help and to cheer the people who are there?

3. What keeps us from obeying God's commands when they come to us? Why do we not always obey our conscience?

4. How can we get a better grip of the Christian faith and of our beliefs so that we can be ready to explain them and defend them to others who question and criticise?

Chapter 18

ANDREW—THE MAN WHO KNEW NO JEALOUSY

In many ways Andrew must have had the loveliest character of all the twelve apostles. He was never one of the most famous of them, but he had a grace upon him that makes him stand out amongst them. It was Andrew's great distinction that he was one of the first two men whom Jesus called to be His followers (John 1:40). He was there right at the very beginning. Now when a man is in things right at the beginning he has a right to expect a special and a leading place, and that is exactly what Andrew never had.

In the four Gospels he is mentioned thirteen times, and six times out of the thirteen he is referred to as *Peter's brother* (e.g. Matthew 4:18; 10:2; Mark 1:16; John 6:8; Luke 6:14). It was Andrew who first brought Peter to Jesus (John 1:41) and ever afterwards Andrew, as it were, lived under the shadow of Peter. When people thought of him they thought of him as the brother of Peter. We would have thought that this must have been hard to bear, but there is never a sign of any word of complaint from this Andrew who had banished jealousy from his heart.

Still further, as we read the Gospels we see that within the circle of the twelve there was an inner circle. There were three disciples whom Jesus took with Him on very special occasions, and these three were Peter, James and John. They were with Jesus at the raising of Jairus' daughter (Mark 5:37); they were with Him on the Mount of Transfiguration (Matthew 17:1); they were with Him in the Garden of Gethsemane (Matthew 26:37). The inner circle is always Peter, James and John. Andrew is not included. It would have been so easy for Andrew to say, "I was Jesus' follower before any of these men. I was one of the first two men who ever gave their lives to Him. It is not fair that I should be pushed into the background and that they should have the special place. I knew Jesus before they did." But never a word of complaint escaped Andrew's lips. Andrew did not know what it was to be jealous.

Jealousy

Jealousy is a terrible thing. If we are jealous it can make ourselves and other people completely wretched. I remember seeing an incident on the football field. There was a team which had a young goalkeeper named McKellar. The team was doing badly and McKellar was rather inexperienced. The team got a new goalkeeper, and on his first appearance the new man played a very fine game. As the teams came off the field at the end of the game, I saw a young man who had been sitting on the touchline run forward and congratulate the new goalkeeper. It was McKellar. He was the first to congratulate the man to whom he had lost his place. That was real sportsmanship, for the real sportsman does not know what it is to be jealous. I remember watching a cricket match between Yorkshire and Scotland. Yardley, the Yorkshire captain, scored a century and the first man to walk forward and congratulate him was the Scottish team captain. That was real sportsmanship because there was no jealousy.

It is very easy to be jealous. If someone gets a favour which we thought we should have got, if someone gets special attention which we thought was our due, if someone gets promotion which we thought we had earned, it is sometimes difficult not to feel hurt and jealous. We must try to remember one thing. It is not we who matter. It is the work, and so long as the work is well done, it does not matter who gets the praise and the credit. We should never be in anything for our own praise and glory, but for the good of the work. Many a boy or man has left the work because he did not get the promotion or the honour he thought he deserved. That is bad Christianity, because the real man harbours no jealousy in his heart.

Andrew brings his Brother

But Andrew was more than merely not jealous. We really

get only three glimpses of Andrew in the gospel story and on each occasion *he is bringing someone to Jesus.*

He began by bringing his brother, Peter. He first found his own brother, Simon, and said to him, "We have found the Messiah" (John 1:41). He had no sooner discovered Jesus for himself than he wanted to bring someone else to Him *and he began at home.* If we discover something good we ought at once to want to share it with others. If we discover an interesting and exciting book we want to tell others about it. We ought to want to share Jesus with others.

A missionary told about a man in India. At first this man was quite hostile to the Church. He actually used to throw stones at it when he was passing the building. Then one day he was attracted by the singing and he went in just by chance. When he heard the story of Jesus it fascinated him. He was not hostile any more; he thought Jesus the loveliest person on earth. He got a Bible and he began to read it, and the Bible, with the wonderful things it told about Jesus and the wonderful promises of God, thrilled him. He used to be reading his Bible and he would come to a bit that moved him and he would run out on to the street and stop the first person he came to and say: "Have you heard about this?" and tell him all about it. He had discovered Jesus himself and he wanted to share Him with others.

No doubt we like our Church. If that is so we should be keen to share it with others. We do not need to be foreign missionaries and to go far away to share things with others. Once a man became a Christian. He went to Spurgeon, the great preacher, and said to him, "I have discovered how wonderful a person Jesus is and I would like to bring someone else to Him. What can I do?" "What's your job?" asked Spurgeon. "I'm an engine driver," the man answered. "Is your fireman a Christian?" demanded Spurgeon. "I don't know," said the man. "Well," said Spurgeon, "start on him." The Church always wants more people. We can start to try to bring into the Church the people we meet every day in life.

Andrew brings a Boy

The next person we see Andrew bringing to Jesus is a boy (John 6:5-14). There was a day when a great crowd of people had followed Jesus out into a lonely place. Evening had come and they were tired and hungry and Jesus did not want to send them off on the road like that, so He suggested that they should be given a meal. The disciples considered a suggestion like that quite hopeless. But there was one exception, and that was Andrew. He knew a lad in the crowd and the lad had a picnic lunch with him, five barley rolls and two little pickled fishes. Andrew told Jesus about him and brought him to Jesus and with that picnic lunch Jesus fed five thousand people. This story tells us a great deal about the character of Andrew.

(*a*) It tells us that Andrew was the kind of man who never considered things hopeless, but who always was willing to do something about it. In this world there are two kinds of people. There are the people who, when they are up against it, sit down and fold their hands and say, "There's nothing to be done." And there are the people who when things are difficult and even look impossible say, "Well, I'll have a shot at something anyhow." Andrew was the second kind of person. If you will look at the names of the people who wrote our hymns you will see that many of the greatest ones were written by Isaac Watts. He wrote "From all that dwell beneath the skies," "I'm not ashamed to own my Lord," "Jesus shall reign where'er the sun," "O God our help in ages past," "When I survey the wondrous Cross," and hundreds of other great hymns. When he was a young man he came home from Church one Sunday and said to his father that he did not think much of the hymns they sang there. Then his father said to him, quite sharply, "Right, if you feel like that, why don't you do something about it?" There and then Isaac Watts started; and every week for the next two years he wrote a new hymn which the congregation sang on Sunday. When we are up against it, there is always something to be done. We should be like Andrew and do it.

(*b*) It tells us that Andrew was an optimist about people. It did not really look as if this boy and his picnic lunch could possibly do much good, but Andrew was an optimist. "Here's a lad," he said to himself. "You never know what he'll be able to do." There was an old German schoolmaster who used to take off his hat to his class of schoolboys every time he came into the class on a morning. People asked him why. He answered, "You never know what one of these boys will be one day." He was right, because Martin Luther was one of them. It is a rule of life that if you let a person see that you think he is no good you make him no good; and if you let a person see that you think he is good you make him good. It is far better to be an optimist than a pessimist about people. Jesus was like that; and Andrew was like that.

(c) Andrew was the kind of man who always tried to do something and the kind of man who was an optimist about people; because above all he was an optimist about Jesus. Most people would have said, "These five rolls and two fishes are no earthly use to feed a crowd like this." But Andrew said, "There are only five rolls and two fishes, but you never know what Jesus can do with them." There is a famous story about a great saint called Saint Theresa. She had the idea that she would like to build a cathedral, but she had only half a crown in money. Someone laughingly said to her, "Not even St. Theresa can do much with half a crown." "No," she said, "but St. Theresa and half a crown *and God* can do anything." It is literally true that we never know what Jesus can do with us and for us. If we give to Jesus what we have and what we are, however little that may be, He can do wonderful things with us. A great singing teacher can make even a person with a quite small voice into a great singer. A great coach can make a person with quite moderate ability into a fine player. A great teacher can make a quite ordinary student into a really good student. Jesus can do things like that, only far more so. Andrew knew that, and when we really believe that, we will make of life something far bigger and better than we ever thought it could be.

Andrew brings the Greeks

But Andrew brought still other people to Jesus. He brought

his brother. He brought the boy. Towards the end of Jesus' life there came certain Greeks to Jerusalem. They wanted to see and to talk with Jesus. They came to Philip and said, "Sir, we wish to see Jesus." They probably came to Philip because Philip is a Greek name. Philip did not know what to do, so he went and told Andrew. Andrew was in no doubt whatever. He took them straight to Jesus (John 12:20-22).

Now there is far more in this than meets the eye. The Jews regarded themselves as God's chosen people, and they thought that God had absolutely no use for any other nation. They actually said that God had created the Gentiles to be fuel for the fires of hell. But Andrew knew better than that; he knew that Jesus wanted everyone to know Him and to love Him, and Andrew was right. One of the most unchristian of all sins is the sin of contempt. Whatever a person is like, however much we may dislike him, however wretched a creature we may think him to be, we must remember that God made him and that Jesus loves and wants him.

There is an old Jewish story. There was a rabbi, called Rabbi Simeon ben Eleazar, who was coming from his teacher's house. He was at the moment feeling very pleased with himself and rather proud. A very ill-favoured man greeted him, but he did not return the greeting. He merely looked at him and said, "Fool! What an ugly creature you are! Are all the men of your town as ugly as you are?" And the man answered, "I do not know. Go and tell the Maker who created me how ugly is the creature He has made."

It is quite wrong to look down on any man, because God is the Maker and the Father of every man, and Jesus loves all men and died to make them His. Andrew knew that and in that he is an example to us.

Andrew

Andrew was the man who banished jealousy from his heart, and who never felt in the least bitter to those who took the place he might have expected to have. He was the man who was always bringing people to Jesus. He began at home by bringing his brother. He brought the boy to Jesus because he always felt that there was something to be done, and because he was an optimist about people and an optimist about Jesus. He brought the Greeks to Jesus because he knew that God has made and loves all men, even the men whom others despise.

QUESTIONS FOR DISCUSSION

1. In what ways can jealousy cause trouble?

2. In what ways can we be optimistic about other people?

3. What kind of people are we apt to despise?